CARRIE UNDERWOOD

CARRIE UNDERWOOD

A Biography

Vernell Hackett

GREENWOOD BIOGRAPHIES

 GREENWOOD

AN IMPRINT OF ABC-CLIO, LLC
Santa Barbara, California • Denver, Colorado • Oxford, England

Copyright 2010 by Vernell Hackett

All rights reserved. No part of this publication may be reproduced, stored in a
retrieval system, or transmitted, in any form or by any means, electronic, mechanical,
photocopying, recording, or otherwise, except for the inclusion of brief quotations in
a review, without prior permission in writing from the publisher.

Library of Congress Cataloging-in-Publication Data

Hackett, Vernell.
    Carrie Underwood : a biography / Vernell Hackett.
        p. cm. — (Greenwood biographies)
    Includes bibliographical references and index.
    ISBN 978-0-313-37851-5 (hard copy : alk. paper) — ISBN 978-0-313-37852-2
(ebook)   1. Underwood, Carrie, 1983–   2. Country musicians—United States—
Biography.   I. Title.
    ML420.U53H33 2010
    782.421642092—dc22   2010024203

ISBN: 978-0-313-37851-5
EISBN: 978-0-313-37852-2

14 13 12 11 10   1 2 3 4 5

This book is also available on the World Wide Web as an eBook.
Visit www.abc-clio.com for details.

Greenwood
An Imprint of ABC-CLIO, LLC

ABC-CLIO, LLC
130 Cremona Drive, P.O. Box 1911
Santa Barbara, California 93116-1911

This book is printed on acid-free paper ∞

Manufactured in the United States of America

CONTENTS

SERIES FOREWORD

In response to high school and public library needs, Greenwood developed this distinguished series of full-length biographies specifically for student use. Prepared by field experts and professionals, these engaging biographies are tailored for high school students who need challenging yet accessible biographies. Ideal for secondary school assignments, the length, format and subject areas are designed to meet educators' requirements and students' interests.

Greenwood offers an extensive selection of biographies spanning all curriculum-related subject areas including social studies, the sciences, literature and the arts, history and politics, as well as popular culture, covering public figures and famous personalities from all time periods and backgrounds, both historic and contemporary, who have made an impact on American and/or world culture. Greenwood biographies were chosen based on comprehensive feedback from librarians and educators. Consideration was given to both curriculum relevance and inherent interest. The result is an intriguing mix of the well known and the unexpected, the saints and sinners from long-ago history and contemporary pop culture. Readers will find a wide array of subject choices from fascinating crime figures like Al Capone to inspiring pioneers like Margaret Mead, from the greatest minds of our time like Stephen Hawking to the most amazing success stories of our day like J.K. Rowling.

While the emphasis is on fact, not glorification, the books are meant to be fun to read. Each volume provides in-depth information about the subject's life from birth through childhood, the teen years, and adulthood. A thorough account relates family background and education, traces personal and professional influences, and explores struggles, accomplishments, and contributions. A timeline highlights the most significant life events against a historical perspective. Bibliographies supplement the reference value of each volume.

PREFACE

Carrie Underwood: A Biography covers the life and career of country singer Carrie Underwood, from her early days in Checotah, Oklahoma, to her current status as one of country music's biggest stars. The book follows Underwood as she began singing in church, then moved on to shows for area civic and music events. Once Underwood decided to try out for *American Idol,* it seemed there was no stopping her. She practically skipped through tryouts before finding herself on her first airplane trip to Hollywood, where she expected to be voted off the show almost immediately. Instead, Underwood found thousands of faithful viewers who voted for her and kept her going to the end, when she and Bo Bice were the only two left standing on the *American Idol* stage. When her name was called as the winner of *Idol's* fourth season, no one was more surprised than Carrie Underwood.

Underwood soon found herself in the middle of a hurricane as she went from winner to recording artist to performing artist in a very few months. The book chronicles all of this as well as the good, bad, and ugly of becoming a country superstar so quickly.

In addition to the story of Underwood's transformation, the book also includes a discography, a list of the singer's awards, a list of music business terms, and suggested further reading. There is also a timeline that gives a miniview of the singer's life and career highlights.

ACKNOWLEDGMENTS

Thanks to the editors and folks at ABC-CLIO for their help in pulling this manuscript together. A huge thanks to friends and colleagues who offered their support while I was writing this biography on Carrie Underwood: Beverly Ross, Brenda McClain, Clark Taylor, Deborah Evans Price, Dorothy Hamm, Henrietta Darr Johnson, Houston Montgomery, John Montgomery, Kim Burns, Liz Cavanaugh, Michelle Honick, Neal Montgomery, Pam Green, Pat Harris, Regina Hoosier, Rita Case, Rob Simbeck, Sarah Brosmer, Skipp Frazier, and others whose names I surely have forgotten. I'll offer the same support for you on your next book! Also thanks to Ken Hackett, without whom I might never have made the move to Nashville to write about country music and all the subsequent topics I have had the privilege to cover.

INTRODUCTION

Carrie Underwood is one of country music's biggest superstars. Underwood won the fourth season of the ultra-popular *American Idol* singing competition on Fox television in May 2005 and went on to become a darling among country music fans. She released her first album, *Some Hearts,* in October 2005. In December 2005, she celebrated gold and platinum status of that album.

Carrie Marie Underwood was born in Checotah, Oklahoma, on March 10, 1983. She attended grade, middle, and high school there, and then enrolled in college at Northeastern State University (NSU) in Tahlequah, Oklahoma. By the time she arrived in college she had been singing professionally for several years, and she continued to do so by performing in the university's variety show, "Downtown Country." She was a journalism major and had hopes of becoming a top-notch journalist. She admits that even though she continued to perform, she had given up her dream of becoming a national recording artist. She joined the Alpha Iota chapter of Sigma Sigma Sigma sorority and was named a runner-up in the Miss NSU beauty pageant in 2004.

Underwood didn't know it, but her dreams were about to come true. Many of her friends encouraged her to try out for *American Idol,* but at first Underwood didn't think much of it. Finally she looked up where the auditions were going to be held, only to discover that the closest one was in St. Louis, eight hours away. Thinking it would be a wasted trip, because she did not believe she would make it past the first audition, Underwood decided not to go. Her mother told her that if she wanted to go, she would drive to St. Louis with her. Underwood thought about it, coming to the realization that if she didn't go to the audition, she might always regret it. Much to her surprise, Underwood not only made it through the first audition, but was soon on her way to the *American Idol* set in Hollywood, where she continued her success right to the end of the show's fourth season.

While her days at *American Idol* were strenuous, they were nothing compared to the days following her win. Underwood was immediately thrust into the world of country music. She won *Idol* in May 2005, and in June she was in Nashville performing at one of country music's largest festival, CMA (Country Music Association) Music Fest. She also taped a performance for "CMT's Greatest Duets" and made her debut on the world-famous *Grand Ole Opry*. During this time she was also listening to songs, trying to find tunes that she wanted to record for her freshman album. In the middle of all this, Underwood was rehearsing for "Pop Tarts Presents American Idols Live! Tour 2005." That tour kicked off on July 12, 2005, in Sunrise, Florida, and ended September 10, 2005, in Syracuse, New York.

While Underwood was on tour, she continued to return to Nashville when she had time to record the songs for her debut album. She also released her first single, "Inside Your Heaven," in June. It was a hectic time for the young woman, who had only recently been a college student. Underwood completed the recording of her album, which was titled *Some Hearts*, and a second single, "Jesus, Take the Wheel," was released. It became her first number-one single and was accepted by country, Christian, and pop audiences.

Underwood released *Some Hearts* in October 2005 and found herself a gold- and platinum-selling artist just two months later, with sales of more than a million units of the album. It went on to become the best-selling debut album by a solo female in country music history. The album produced two more singles, "Wasted," and the very popular "Before He Cheats." The latter song showed another side of Underwood, one in which the woman who is cheated on gets her revenge. Underwood said that while she wasn't like that, it was fun to try and play a part that was so totally opposite her personal character.

While her album was selling millions of copies, Underwood went out on her first national concert tours with a couple of major country artists. Brad Paisley was the first entertainer to take her on the road, followed by Kenny Chesney. Underwood had performed in Oklahoma, in the area surrounding her hometown, but these were the first major tours she had been on in which she played directly to the country audience. She had two major entertainers to learn from, and she has often said how much she learned from these two performers who took her under their wing.

When Underwood's *Some Hearts* was released in October, the singer was in New York City performing on her first major awards show, the 39th annual CMA Awards, which is affiliated with the Country Music Association. An excited Underwood went out at midnight and bought a copy of her album, then performed on the show that evening. While she was not nominated for an award in 2005, Underwood went on to have many nominations for the Country Music Association awards as well as many others.

Underwood received her first major award nomination from the Academy of Country Music in March 2006, for Top Female Vocalist, Top New Female, and Single Record of the Year for "Jesus, Take the Wheel." The single was also nominated for Song of the Year. A week later she was nominated for three Country Music Television video awards, Breakthrough Video, Most Inspiring, and Female Video, all for "Jesus, Take the Wheel." Her first major award win was for CMT's Female Video and Breakthrough Video. On May 23, Underwood took home two wins from the ACM (Academy of Country Music) awards, Top New Female Vocalist, and Single of the Year for "Jesus, Take the Wheel." Many more awards followed for the young singer in her career, including Grammys, People's Choice, and CMA Awards (CMAs).

While Underwood was making a huge splash on the national scene, she remained a hometown hero in Checotah. In December 2005, the singer was named *Oklahoma Magazine*'s Oklahoman of the Year. In April of the following year she was inducted into the Hall of Fame of her alma mater, Northeastern State University in Tahlequah, Oklahoma. In May of that year, Underwood finally got her college degree, graduating magna cum laude with a B.S. degree. She returned to Oklahoma on her first major tour in June 2006, performing at Country Fever in Pryor.

The media is always quick to jump on a story, as Underwood found out soon into her career. On April 10, 2006, while at a press conference for the CMA Awards, Wynonna Judd was asked about Carrie, who had just won her first major award. Judd admitted that she didn't know a lot about the newcomer but thought she had a great voice. She then went on to talk about the vanilla singers in country music, which many people interpreted as a comment on Carrie. Judd was quick to set the record straight, coming back into the media room to tell the group of journalists that wasn't at all what she meant, but the story made its way around the blogs and other media sites for a few days following the incident.

A similar incident happened in 2006 at the CMA Awards. After the announcement was made that Underwood had won Female Vocalist, cameras panning the event caught Faith Hill mouthing "What?" People interpreted this as a show of dismay because she did not win. The next day Hill issued a statement through her publicist stating, "The idea that I would act disrespectful towards a fellow musician is unimaginable to me." She and Underwood talked, and the Oklahoma native told her fans via her Web site that she never thought Hill had meant any disrespect. The incident also made the rounds of media outlets for a few days before it was lost to the next piece of juicy news.

In 2008, Underwood co-headlined her first tour. She and international country star Keith Urban joined forces for the "Love, Pain & the Whole Crazy Carnival Ride Tour," which kicked off January 31 in Uncasville, Connecticut. At the same time, Underwood was preparing for her first headline tour, "Carnival Ride," which opened May 2 in Tucson, Arizona.

Underwood discovered early in her career that her private life was no longer private. If she even had dinner with a member of the opposite sex, tabloids predicted the two were dating. When she actually did date, every move was made known to the world, and when she broke up, it was even worse. When Underwood began dating Canadian hockey star Mike Fisher, all that came to an end, as the two announced their engagement in December 2009. Their wedding was held July 10, 2010, at the Ritz Carlton Reynolds Plantation in Greensboro, Georgia.

Underwood continues her headline status, opening her "Play On" tour March 11, 2010, in Reading, Pennsylvania. She returns to *American Idol* often to perform and is seldom off the list of nominees and winners for awards. On January 12, 2010, her *Carnival Ride* CD was certified triple-platinum, for three million dollars in sales. Two days later, *Play On* was certified Gold and Platinum simultaneously, representing one million units sold. She made her acting debut on March 1 in an episode of CBS's *How I Met Your Mother*. She headed for the silver screen later in the year, filming *Soul Surfer* in Hawaii. She plays the part of youth leader Sarah Hill, who was a great friend to one-armed surfing champion Bethany Hamilton, whom the movie is about.

TIMELINE: EVENTS IN THE LIFE OF CARRIE UNDERWOOD

March 10, 1983	Carrie Marie Underwood is born in Muskogee, Oklahoma.
2001	Graduates from Checotah (OK) High School as salutatorian.
January 19, 2005	Auditions for *American Idol* in St. Louis, Missouri.
February 22, 2005	Top 12 girls perform on *American Idol*.
March 22, 2005	*American Idol* judge Simon Cowell predicts Carrie will win.
May 25, 2005	Wins fourth season of *American Idol*.
June 8, 2005	Tapes "CMT's Greatest Duets."
June 9, 2005	Performs at the Coliseum Show at CMA Music Festival.
June 10, 2005	Makes her *Grand Ole Opry* Debut.
June 14, 2005	Single "Inside Your Heaven" is released.
July 12, 2005	40-city "Pop Tarts Presents American Idols Live! Tour 2005" kicks off at the Home Depot Center in Sunrise, Florida.
July 26, 2005	"Inside Your Heaven" is certified a Gold single.
September 17, 2005	"CMT's Greatest Duets" airs.

September 24, 2005	Wins Tulsa, Oklahoma's Spot Music Awards Artist of the Year.
October 18, 2005	Second single, "Jesus, Take the Wheel," is released.
October 27, 2005	Makes surprise appearance at Oklahoma Music Hall of Fame Awards ceremony.
November 15, 2005	Album, *Some Hearts*, is released. Performs "Jesus, Take The Wheel" on the 39th annual CMA Awards show, held at Madison Square Garden in New York City.
November 18, 2005	"Inside Your Heaven" single is certified Gold for Digital Downloads.
December 9, 2005	*Some Hearts* is certified Gold and Platinum simultaneously.
December 11, 2005	Performs for President George W. Bush for "Christmas in Washington" special on TNT.
December 14, 2005	TNT airs "Christmas in Washington" special with Carrie, Rascal Flatts, and others.
December 26, 2005	Named *Oklahoma Magazine*'s Oklahoman of the Year.
January 6, 2006	*Some Hearts* is certified double Platinum.
January 25, 2006	"Jesus, Take the Wheel" is certified Gold single.
February 15, 2007	Tops the *Billboard* country singles chart for the sixth week in a row with "Jesus, Take the Wheel."
March 2, 2006	Returns to *American Idol*, this time as a special guest, and performs "Jesus, Take the Wheel."
March 8, 2006	Gets her first major awards nomination, Top Female Vocalist, Top New Female, and Single Record of the Year for "Jesus, Take the Wheel," from the Academy of Country Music. Her single, "Jesus, Take the Wheel," is also nominated for Song of the Year, with award to her and songwriters Brett James, Hillary Lindsey, and Gordon Sampson.
March 15, 2006	Nominated for three CMT Awards—Breakthrough Video, Most Inspiring Video, and Female Video, all for "Jesus, Take the Wheel."

April 10, 2006   Wins two CMT Video Awards, Female Video and Breakthrough Video, both for "Jesus, Take the Wheel."

April 10, 2006   Wynonna Judd is asked about Carrie and admits she doesn't know a lot about her but thinks she has a great voice. She then goes on to talk about the vanilla singers in country music, which many people interpret as a comment on Carrie.

April 28, 2006   Inducted into the Hall of Fame of her alma mater, Northeastern State University in Tahlequah, Oklahoma. She finds out her album, *Some Hearts*, has been certified triple Platinum.

May 6, 2006   Graduates magna cum laude with a B.S. degree from Northeastern State University in Tahlequah, Oklahoma.

May 23, 2006   Wins Top New Female Vocalist and Single of the Year for "Jesus, Take the Wheel," at the Academy of Country Music Awards.

May 24, 2006   Performs "Don't Forget To Remember Me" on the finale of season five on *American Idol*.

June 8, 2006   Makes first appearance as a major-label recording artist in Oklahoma at Country Fever in Pryor.

August 30, 2006   Secures four nominations for the Country Music Association Awards—Female Vocalist, Single, and Music Video, both for "Jesus, Take the Wheel," and Horizon Award.

September 19, 2006   Has two nominations for American Music Awards, Favorite Female Country and Favorite New Artist, all genres.

September 23, 2006   Included as part of the double CD, *Oklahoma Rising*, sponsored by the Oklahoma Centennial Commission.

November 6, 2006   *Some Hearts* is certified quadruple Platinum, and Carrie wins Female Vocalist and Horizon Award from the Country Music Association.

November 7, 2006	Nominated for two People's Choice Awards—Favorite Female Singer and Favorite Country Song for "Before He Cheats."
November 19, 2006	Plays Tulsa's Expo Square Pavilion as part of her "Some Hearts" tour
November 21, 2006	Walks away with Favorite New Artist in the all-genre category of the American Music Awards.
December 7, 2006	Gets two Grammy nominations, for Best Female Country Vocal Performance for "Jesus, Take the Wheel," and Best New Artist.
December 13, 2006	Begins first USO tour, an eight-day trek through Iraq and Kuwait.
January 5, 2007	*Some Hearts* is certified quintuple-Platinum.
January 9, 2007	Wins Favorite Female Singer and Favorite Country Song for "Before He Cheats" at 33rd annual People's Choice Awards.
February 11, 2007	Wins two awards at 49th annual Grammy awards, Best New Artist and Best Female Country Vocal Performance, for "Jesus, Take the Wheel."
February 22, 2007	"Before He Cheats" is certified Gold as a digital single.
February 28, 2007	Earns three nods for CMT Video Awards: Best Video and Best Female Video for "Before He Cheats," plus Video with the Best Direction.
March 6, 2007	Nominated for ACM Awards: Top Female Vocalist, Top Album for *Some Hearts*, Single Record, Song of the Year, and Top Video, all for "Before He Cheats."
March 8, 2007	Returns for *American Idol* performance to sing "Wasted."
March 24, 2007	Guests for the first time on *Saturday Night Live*.
April 16, 2007	Wins three awards at CMT Video Awards for Bests Video, Best Female Video, and Video with the Best Direction, all for "Before He Cheats."
May 3, 2007	*Some Hearts* is certified for sales of sextuple Platinum.

May 5, 2007	Wins three times at the 42nd annual ACM Awards: Top Female Vocalist, Top Album for *Some Hearts*, Top Video for "Before He Cheats."
May 23, 2007	"Before He Cheats" earns Platinum digital certification.
July 30, 2007	"So Small" is released as single.
August 7, 2007	Nominated for MTV Video Music Awards' Best New Artist for "Before He Cheats."
August 30, 2007	Nominated for three CMA awards: Female Vocalist, Single, and Video for "Before He Cheats."
October 9, 2007	Nominated for Favorite Country Female Vocalist and Favorite Country Album for *Some Hearts* for the American Music Awards.
October 23, 2007	Second album, *Carnival Ride*, is released.
November 7, 2007	Wins two awards at 41st annual CMA Awards show: Female Vocalist and Single of the Year for "Before He Cheats."
November 16, 2007	Performs on Oklahoma's Centennial Spotlight final spectacular.
November 18, 2007	Wins two awards at American Music Awards, Favorite Country Female and Favorite Country Album for *Some Hearts*.
December 10, 2007	"All-American Girl" released as a single.
December 11, 2007	Nominated for Best Female Vocal Performance for "Before He Cheats," and Best Country Collaboration with Vocals with Brad Paisley for "Oh Love" at the 50th annual Grammy awards.
December 13, 2007	*Carnival Ride* is certified Gold, Platinum, and Double Platinum on the same day.
December 31, 2007	Performs on "Dick Clark's Rockin' New Year's Eve."
January 31, 2008	"Jesus, Take the Wheel" is certified as a Platinum single, and "Before He Cheats" is certified double Platinum.
February 10, 2008	"Before He Cheats" wins Best Female Country Vocal Performance at the 50th annual Grammy awards.

February 13, 2008	"Wasted" and "So Small" are certified digital singles.
February 18, 2008	Opens first night of her first headlining "Carnival Ride Tour" in Wilkes-Barre, Pennsylvania.
March 10, 2008	"Last Name" is released as a single.
March 15, 2008	Is invited to become a member of Grand Ole Opry.
March 21, 2008	Meets Mike Fisher of the Ottawa Senators professional hockey team for the first time.
May 10, 2008	Becomes a member of the Grand Ole Opry.
July 7, 2008	"Just A Dream" is released as a single.
October 22, 2008	A wax likeness is placed at the world-famous Madam Tussauds Wax Museum in New York City.
November 10, 2008	Is nominated for three People's Choice Awards: Favorite Female, Favorite Song for "Last Name," and Favorite Star under 35.
November 12, 2008	Wins Female Vocalist at the 42nd CMA Awards Show; cohosts the show for the first time with Brad Paisley.
November 23, 2008	Wins Favorite Country Album for *Carnival Ride* at the American Music Awards.
December 4, 2008	Nominated for Best Female Country Vocal Performance for "Last Name."
January 7, 2009	Wins three times at the People's Choice Awards: Favorite Female, Favorite Song for "Last Name," and Favorite Star under 35.
January 12, 2009	"I Told You So," a remake of the old Randy Travis hit, is released as a single.
February 8, 2009	Wins Best Female Country Vocal Performance for "Last Name" at 51st annual Grammy Awards.
March 5, 2009	Nominated for Entertainer of the Year, Female Vocalist of the Year, Album of the Year for *Carnival Ride*, and Video of the Year "Just a Dream" for the ACM Awards.

March 17, 2009	"I Told You So" released as a duet single with Randy Travis, who had the first hit with the tune.
March 19, 2009	Receives Gold Single certification for "Just a Dream" and "Last Name."
March 24 2009	Receives Gold Single certification for "All-American Dream."
April 5, 2009	Wins Entertainer of the Year and Top Female Vocalist at the 44th annual Academy of Country Music Awards.
May 18, 2009	Named as one of *Forbes* magazine's top earning *American Idol* winners.
June 4, 2009	"I Told You So" is certified Gold.
June 11, 2009	"Carrie Underwood: All American Girl" exhibit opens at Country Music Hall of Fame in Nashville.
September 9, 2009	Nominated for Female Vocalist and Vocal Event with Randy Travis for "I Told You So" for the CMA Awards.
October 16, 2009	Travels to Singapore for the first time to perform at the opening of the Ion Orchard mall.
November 3, 2009	Third album, *Play On*, is released.
November 10, 2009	Nominated for Favorite Female Artist and Favorite Country Artist for People's Choice Awards.
November 11, 2009	Cohosts 43rd CMA Awards show with Brad Paisley for the second time.
November 23, 2009	"Temporary Home" released as single.
November 26, 2009	Performs on "CNN Heroes: An All Star Tribute."
December 7, 2009	Hosts "Carrie Underwood: An All-Star Holiday Special" on Fox with special guests Dolly Parton, Brad Paisley, and others.
December 12, 2009	Receives Harmony Award during the annual Nashville Symphony Ball.
December 20, 2009	Becomes engaged to Mike Fisher of the Ottawa Senators professional hockey team.

January 5, 2010	"Cowboy Casanova" single is certified Gold.
January 6, 2010	Wins Favorite Country Artist at People's Choice Awards.
January 31, 2010	Picks up fifth Grammy, Best Country Collaboration with Vocals, for "I Told You So" with Randy Travis.
February 7, 2010	Sings National Anthem at Super Bowl XLIV, which pits the Indianapolis Colts against the New Orleans Saints.
February 11, 2010	Makes debut as "Carrie Underworm" singing "The Worm Anthem" on PBS series *Sesame Street*.
February 2010	Begins filming supporting role in movie *Soul Surfer*, as good friend of 19-year old surfer Bethany Hamilton, who despite losing an arm in a shark attack continued to compete as a professional surfer.
March 1, 2010	Makes debut as actress on CBS's *How I Met Your Mother*.
March 2, 2010	Receives six nominations for the Academy of Country Music Awards—Entertainer of the Year, Female Vocalist of the Year, Album of the Year for *Play On*, Vocal Event of the Year with Randy Travis for "I Told You So," and as the artist and the songwriter for Song of the Year for "Cowboy Casanova" with cowriters Mike Elizondo and Brett James.
March 11, 2010	"Play On" tour kicks off in Reading, Pennsylvania, with special guests Craig Morgan and Sons of Sylvia.
April 18, 2010	Attends Academy of Country Music Awards in Las Vegas, which airs live over CBS-TV. Makes Academy of Country Music history when she becomes first woman to win the coveted Entertainer of the Year award twice. Also presented Triple Crown award for having previously won Best New Artist, Female Vocalist and Entertainer.

Chapter 1

CRAZY DREAMS

People driving down Interstate 40 near U.S. Route 69 in the first years of the new millennium usually drove right past the exit to Checotah, Oklahoma, without a second glance, unless they had a specific reason to go to the sleepy little farm town. That all changed on May 25, 2005, when Checotah native Carrie Underwood was named the winner of season four of Fox Network's popular show *American Idol*. No longer was the small Oklahoma town an unknown, because as Underwood's popularity increased, so did the identity of Checotah. The town leaders furthered its popularity by erecting a sign declaring it "Home of Carrie Underwood" on August 10, 2005. They understood that fans of the *Idol* winner wanted to know all about her, and that included information about where she grew up and started her singing career.

Carrie Marie Underwood was born March 10, 1983 in Muskogee, Oklahoma. Her parents, Stephen and Carole Underwood, took their daughter home from Muskogee Regional Medical Center to Checotah, where her two older sisters, Shanna and Stephanie, anxiously awaited her arrival. Shanna, who is 13 years Underwood's senior, moved away when her younger sister was 4, but the two have remained close. Stephanie is 10 years older than her younger sister. The family lived on a farm outside the town, although Mr. Underwood was not a farmer. He worked as a paper mill operator for Georgia-Pacific for 30 years, and Mrs. Underwood is a retired elementary school teacher.

The area started out as a farming community long before the name Checote Switch was introduced. Pre-Columbian tribes grew corn, squash, and beans in the area before the white people began to move into the territory. Once cattle drives became the popular way to move livestock north, the Texas Road (now Highway 69) became a major trail used to bring cattle and sheep into the area. This also brought ranchers to Checotah, offering settlers another means to make a living in the area. Both farming and ranching remain vital to Checotah today.

The Checotah area also became the home of the Creek Nation after the Five Civilized Tribes were relocated from the Eastern states to Indian Territory between 1830 and 1840. African Americans arrived during the same time period. Settlers found their lives in turmoil during the Civil War, with the Battle of Honey Springs, won by the Union Army, fought northeast of the town on July 17, 1863.

American Idol *winner Carrie Underwood, right, is presented with a replica of a road sign to be placed in her hometown of Checotah, Oklahoma, by Oklahoma governor Brad Henry, right, and Oklahoma first lady Kim Henry, left, at a news conference at the state capitol in Oklahoma City, August 10, 2005. (AP Photo.)*

The town of Checotah was born after the Civil War, during the period of Reconstruction. It is named after the Creek Indian chief, soldier, and statesman, Samuel Checote. The M.K.T. Railroad saw fit to honor the chief in 1872 when the company built its rail line south through Indian Territory. They called the area Checote Switch, which was shortened to Checotah as the town grew. The railroad opened the area as a central post where agricultural products were shipped to other regions of the country.

Today trains no longer stop in Checotah, whose population has remained constant since 1980 at around 3,500, and the old railway depot is now a museum. Nevertheless, farming and ranching remain a viable part of the local community as it strives to offer its young men and women a way to earn a living. Checotah is a relatively safe town, with no murders reported from 2001 through 2007. Burglaries, assaults, and theft were the most often-named crimes during that timeframe. The weather might actually prove more hazardous than crime. While the area has only two to three inches of snow during its winter storms, it is an area with high tornado activity.

Underwood had a typical childhood, one in which she discovered a love for music early in life. Both of her parents were supportive, though her mother may have been more verbal with encouraging words than her father, who remained the strong silent type as Underwood made her way through early performances and found ways to get in front of the public to sing. It was apparent even when she was a youngster that she was going to be a singer—her parents have pictures of her singing into hairbrushes and anything else that she could use as a microphone so she could pretend to be performing onstage.

Underwood says her family provided her with a stable background, with parents who worked hard to provide for their children. She told Westwood One Radio Network, "My parents started out both very poor and they made great lives for themselves and great lives for my sisters and me, so I respect and love my parents, and I love my sisters and my friends. I'm lucky to have all those people in my life."[1]

The singer never knew all of her grandparents or great-grandparents. She was asked by AOL's www.theboot.com who she would like to have dinner with, living or dead, and she chose family members who had passed on. "I really didn't know my dad's dad, and my dad was the last of six boys. I never met my great-grandparents and really didn't know the one side of my grandparents really well. I'd just like to know where I came from so I'd pick somebody from my past that I never got the chance to have a conversation with or know what they looked like."[2] While her parents realized their daughter enjoyed performing, Underwood says her mother was never a stage mom. She maintains that they let her grow up by supporting her and loving her and helping her as best they could.

One of the places where Underwood learned to sing was the Free Will Baptist Church in Checotah, which she attended with her parents. She began singing in church when she was three years old, belting out traditional tunes like "How Great Thou Art" and other hymns. Her faith in God remains strong today, as she believes that God bestows everyone with a particular talent and then presents them with opportunities to use those talents.

While competing on *American Idol,* Underwood told the *Tulsa World* that she appreciated the time spent singing in her hometown church. In fact, she went so far as to say that she would have to use everything she learned as a little girl singing in that church to win the competition. "There were a couple of times when I'd look out at the people sitting out there and kind of realize that, you know, I was, I guess, making a difference and touching some people. I mean, I totally believe that my voice came from God. That's where my talent comes from. I always want to make sure that I give back any way I can."[3]

Despite her church upbringing, Underwood admitted to the newspaper that she was happy when another *Idol* contestant would be booted from the show instead of her, although she added that she felt a bit ashamed of her feelings. "I feel kind of guilty because so-and-so is not going to be here anymore, but I'm glad it's not me," she said. "I feel guilty but I guess you kind of get used to it after a while."[4]

One of the places where Underwood wouldn't sing was Sam and Ella's Pizza Joint in Tahlequah, Oklahoma, where she worked as a waitress. "She would never sing for us because she was too shy," head waiter Benjamin Bantista told the *Tulsa World.* "She was a good waitress, though."[5]

Evidence of Underwood's former tenure at the pizza place includes a Vitamin Water ad featuring her face and a pizza paddle bearing musical notes and Carrie's name, which hangs on the wall by the restaurant's door. Bantista said people come in for the food, but that it's also good for the restaurant that they can say she worked there. He informed the newspaper that the former employee and her sorority sisters from Sigma Sigma Sigma had come in a few months prior, when she was in town for recognition from the "Downtown Country" music troupe. He said she's always welcome to stop by and added, "If that singing thing don't work out, she can always come back."[6]

While Underwood's family was supportive of her musical endeavors, some of her classmates didn't understand her passion. Thus the singer often sought to perform outside of Checotah instead of looking for performance opportunities in her hometown. She says that unless she was performing in church, or fulfilling a few special requests to perform in Checotah, she didn't sing anywhere near her hometown because the kids made fun of her interest in music. Underwood instead would travel to towns like Stillwell to perform in the town's 54th annual Strawberry Festival or to Tulsa for Darryl Starbird's 39th annual National Rod and Custom Car Show and Monster Truck Races. In 2003 she opened for country singer Doug Stone at Oklahoma's oldest festival, the 71st annual Rooster Days in Broken Arrow, Oklahoma. She also opened for a number of other artists including Diamond Rio, The Wilkinson's, Exile, Gene Watson, Billy Hoffman, and Earl Thomas Conley. The singer doesn't look at those times as anything anymore difficult than other youngsters have to go through when they are in high school; she points out that there are always those who find a way to make life miserable for someone else because of what they do, the clothes they wear, or the fact that they aren't in a particular clique.

Even when she was just starting out, Underwood always tried to instill positive messages to fans when she signed autographs after her shows. Often, especially when giving out her soon-to-be famous signature for school-age fans, she would add "Follow your dreams" after her autograph, according to fellow Checotah native Jennifer LeMasters, who later designed a billboard honoring the singer that was placed at the entrance to their hometown.[7]

While growing up, Underwood had a number of interesting places to go in the Checotah area. She could familiarize herself with local history by visiting the Sharpe House, Indian Territory Cemetery, Honey

Springs Civil War Battlefield, and the 1903 IOOF (International Order of Odd Fellows, a men's association) Home. Other activities she could take part in were the numerous rodeo events, or she could explore nearby Eufaula Lake and the land around it.

Underwood is in good company when it comes to celebrities hailing from Checotah and surrounding areas. Other recognized names from the area include Belle Star, "Queen of the Bandits," country singer Mel McDaniel, the late Pulitzer Prize–winning war correspondent Jim G. Lucas, and Silver Star recipient Paul H. Carr, the World War II naval hero for whom the USS *Carr* is named. Other fellow Oklahomans who followed their dreams to Nashville include Vince Gill, Reba McEntire, Garth Brooks, Toby Keith, and Ronnie Dunn of Brooks & Dunn.

When Underwood wanted to venture out to a bigger city than Checotah, she could travel 40 miles to Broken Arrow, with a population of 50,000; take a 50-mile drive to Tulsa, which boasted 200,000; or cross the border into Texas, traveling 200 miles to Dallas, with one million residents within its boundaries. More than likely she visited nearby cities with exotic names like Shady Grove, Oktaha, Duchess Landing, or Council Hill, all within a five-mile area of her hometown.

In 1996, at the age of 13, she was offered a recording deal by Capitol Records in Nashville. This was the same year that LeAnn Rimes, then 14, hit the national country charts with the hit song "Blue." Rimes's success was the first time a teenager had graced the country music charts with a national hit since Tanya Tucker released "Delta Dawn" in 1972. When there is a breakthrough act such as Rimes, other record labels look for similar singers who can bring comparable success for their company.

If the contract had been signed, Underwood would have been given the opportunity to go to Nashville and record songs for release to country radio. As often happens in the music industry, changes in personnel in the Capitol Records Nashville office resulted in the contract not being signed. The singer did record a demo while she was there, but she told the Associated Press during her *Idol* competition that she didn't like listening to that recording anymore because she sounded like a little kid. She admitted that she had hopes of being the next LeAnn Rimes but added, "I honestly think it's a lot better that nothing came out of it now, because I wouldn't have been ready then. Like I said, everything has a way of working out. Obviously there was a reason that that didn't happen."[8]

Two years later Underwood was again in Nashville, taking voice lessons from renowned vocal coach Renee Grant-Williams. Although Underwood had no idea that in seven years she would be competing on the television show *American Idol,* she connected with a coach who worked with several of the show's contestants over the years. Grant-Williams's philosophy when it comes to teaching people to sing is to work with their natural abilities, not try and change the way they sound to make them into another kind of singer entirely. She works with the client on breathing techniques and voice control to enable them to be better singers in the studio and during onstage performances.

Throughout high school Underwood was very serious about having a career as a recording artist and performer. She graduated as salutatorian from Checotah High School, which has around 500 students in the four-year facility, grades 9 through 12. Underwood will probably never forget her graduation night in 2001, and not just because of the honor she was receiving. It seems the spunky high school graduate delivered her salutatorian address with a black eye. Underwood had not been in a fight; she just got in the way of a stray softball a few days before the ceremony. Teachers remember Underwood as a student who was always attentive to being the best she could be in both school studies and her musical activities. Checotah High School principal Pam Keeter told the Associated Press that Underwood was smart, polite, and respectful.[9]

Underwood decided to continue her education and enrolled at Northeastern State University in Tahlequah, Oklahoma. There she became a mass communications major. She also joined Sigma Sigma Sigma sorority. Sororities are organizations for women that give them a circle of friends on campus, creating lifelong bonds among their members. While this is one of Sigma's purposes, the organization also strives to develop strong womanly character and promote high standards of conduct within its ranks. The organization's foundation distributes funds for charitable, philanthropic, educational, and other benevolent purposes. It seeks to focus its programs on enhancing the leadership skills of modern-day women, providing grants and scholarships to students, and supporting play therapy programs for children. Underwood says she joined the sorority because she felt lonely at the university without her high school friends, who had chosen other colleges to attend. She credits the new friends she found at Sigma with helping bring her out of her shell.

For two years Underwood performed in the university's "Downtown Country" show in Tahlequah during the summer. The singer also competed in several campus beauty pageants, being named runner-up in the Miss NSU competition in 2004.

With just three credits left before she would receive her degree, Underwood left college in 2004 to compete on *American Idol*. The 23-year-old decided to pursue her dream of becoming a nationally known singer. A year after she won the talent show, on May 6, 2006, she graduated from NSU magna cum laude with a bachelor's degree in mass communication with an emphasis in journalism. Just a few weeks earlier, on April 28, 2006, she became a member of Northeastern State University's Hall of Fame.

Despite her instant climb to fame, Underwood was determined to get her college degree. She credits her time at college for laying the foundation for the rest of her life; in addition, she is secure in the fact that she has a degree that offers her the opportunity to pursue another career that she loves, interviewing and writing about the celebrities who are her peers.

NOTES

1. Vernell Hackett, Carrie Underwood Interview, Westwood One Radio Network, October 2, 2007.

2. Deborah Evans Price, Carrie Underwood Interview: 11 Questions, www.theboot.com, http://www.theboot.com/2009/10/21/carrie-underwood-interview-11-questions/, October 21, 2009.

3. Matt Gleason, "Coming Clean," *Tulsa World*, March 20, 2005.

4. Ibid.

5. Cary Aspinwall, "Shy Down-Home Waitress Blossoms Into Superstar," *Tulsa World*, October 29, 2008.

6. Ibid.

7. John Wooley, "Carrie Country," *Tulsa World*, May 26, 2005.

8. Associated Press, "Carrie Underwood has her Town Talking," http://today.msnbc.msn.com/id/7794328/#ixzz0rF1pfMRo, May 9, 2005.

9. Ibid.

Chapter 2

I AIN'T IN CHECOTAH ANYMORE

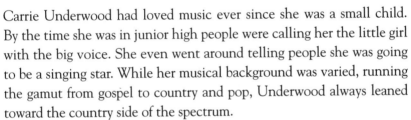

Carrie Underwood had loved music ever since she was a small child. By the time she was in junior high people were calling her the little girl with the big voice. She even went around telling people she was going to be a singing star. While her musical background was varied, running the gamut from gospel to country and pop, Underwood always leaned toward the country side of the spectrum.

Although Underwood dreamed of becoming a singer, the more practical side took over after she finished high school and she was enrolled at Northeastern State University. In a bio written for her *Carnival Ride* album, Underwood said, "After high school I pretty much gave up on the dream of singing. I had reached a point in my life where I had to be practical and prepare for my future in the 'real world'."[1]

It might have been her intent to leave music behind, but it continued to follow her even after Underwood arrived at Northeastern in Tahlequah, Oklahoma, with the intent of majoring in broadcast journalism. The young woman continued to perform, produced a student-run television series, and penned stories for *The Northeastern*, the university's newspaper. She also took part in a country music show, "Downtown Country," a variety-style show where she steeped herself even more in the traditions of country stars like Patsy Cline and the Carter Family. It was also while singing in this show that she learned to perform before a crowd. She was named a runner-up in the Miss NSU beauty pageant in 2004.

At the end of 2004, in her fourth year of college, friends began to encourage Underwood to audition for a television show that had caught the fancy of America's television audience, as well as many singers who wanted to use that vehicle to stardom. *American Idol* had become one of the highest-rated shows on television, capturing an audience of more than 25 million viewers. The show's concept was simple: singers auditioned in cities and towns around the country in a kind of pre-*Idol* competition. Some made it and others went away crushed by the experience. Those who made it went on to the next round, and the next round, until finally they were flown to Los Angeles to compete against other singers, all of whom wanted to become the next "American Idol."

Underwood saw an ad for the auditions for *American Idol* while watching television one night. She checked the audition schedule and found that the closest audition to her was in St. Louis, Missouri, an eight-hour drive from Checotah. She decided that was too far to go for what she was certain would be a wasted trip, but her mother offered to drive her to the audition if she wanted to try out. At first the young college student said no; then after thinking about it she had a change of heart. Underwood began to realize that if she didn't make the effort to audition, she would graduate from college, get a job, have a family, and never know what would have happened if she had given it a try. Perhaps she remembered her own philosophy: God gives people talent and then opportunities to use that talent. *American Idol* became Underwood's opportunity.

Once the decision was made, the singer moved quickly. The audition in St. Louis was on Sunday, August 8, 2004, which meant she and her mother would have to leave after her performance on the "Downtown Country" show in Tahlequah. Immediately after the show was over, Underwood and her mother headed to the Edward Jones Dome in St. Louis, Missouri, and her destiny. Mother and daughter drove all night, arriving just two hours before the 8 A.M. call time for interested parties to receive wristbands that would make them eligible for the auditions. It was another eight hours before Underwood belted out the Martina McBride hit, "Phones Are Ringing All Over Town," a song written by

David Mackechnie, Kin Vassy, and Marc Beeson, for *Idol*'s supervising producer James Breen. She later told the judges that McBride was her favorite singer.

Underwood didn't think she sang very well and expected the experience to be over. Instead she was asked to come back the next day to sing for the show's executive producer, Nigel Lythgoe. She chose another McBride song, "Independence Day," written by Gretchen Peters. For her third and final round, Underwood performed the Bonnie Raitt classic, "I Can't Make You Love Me," written by Nashville songwriters Mike Reid and Allen Shamblin. This time she performed for the *American Idol* judges, Simon Cowell, Randy Jackson, and Paula Abdul. She admitted to the three that she was nervous and said Cowell was "scary." The singer also said she chose "I Can't Make You Love Me" because she wanted to do a song that the judges didn't hear over and over during the early stages of the competition. Cowell stopped her in the middle of the song and said it was very good. They asked her to do her "chicken thing," which she did, making the sound of a chicken clucking. Laughing, she commented, "I could have just clucked my way into 'American Idol' couldn't I?"[2] The judges laughed in response to her statement, and Cowell commented that he had been surprised they had never had a good country singer on *American Idol*. All three judges thought enough of her performance to send her on to the competition. On January 29, 2005, *American Idol* showed Underwood's audition. It was the first time the *Idol* audience got to see the young woman from Checotah, Oklahoma, but it definitely wasn't their last.

When Underwood walked onboard for that airplane ride to Hollywood, it was her first time in the air. She told *Esquire* magazine about driving to the airport to make that historic flight. "I was so nervous when I was on my way to L.A. I'd never been on a plane, and I was going alone. I kind of got teary-eyed. My dad was driving (to the airport), and he said, 'If you want to go home, we can go home, and you never have to think about this again.' And I thought, if I don't go, I'm choosing for this not to happen. It will be my choice. So I figured it would be easier for me to get kicked off 'American Idol' than to have it be my own decision."[3]

Thousands of hopefuls entered regional auditions for *American Idol* from across the country. Out of those, only 193 got to go to Hollywood.

Another 44 took another step closer to *Idol* stardom, with the final 12 contestants chosen from those.

Underwood made it through to that final dozen and carried herself through, staying in the competition every week of *Idol's* season four broadcast, which premiered on January 18, 2005. *American Idol* is not an easy competition to go through. Not only are the contestants under the constant scrutiny of the judges, they go through a lot of behind-the-scenes rehearsals and training that keeps them going at a pace that would rival any 40-hour-a-week job. Once the rehearsals were over and Underwood walked onstage, it was up to her to impress the judges and the audience that would vote each week.

The singer described being on *American Idol* as boot camp to CMA *Close Up*. While it might have been hard to hear the judges' critiques, some positive and many negative, she is quick to say the show's sink-or-swim ethic helped her win the competition. "There was nobody to tell me what I should sing, or what to do, and being away from my friends and family, pretty much on my own, I had to grow up. If I could survive that and not go crazy then I could survive everything that followed. It so prepared me for what I do now."[4]

During the weeks of competition, Underwood chose a variety of songs from various styles to perform for the judges. Among her choices were Shania Twain's "Man I Feel Like a Woman," the Dixie Chicks's "Sin Wagon," and Rascal Flatts's "Bless The Broken Road." The young woman included music from pop genres like Janis Joplin's "Piece of My Heart," Jordin Sparks's "Love Is a Battlefield" and Air Supply's "Making Love out of Nothing at All." She leaned heavily to the country side in her choices, including Jo Dee Messina's "Because You Love Me," the Everly Brothers's "When Will I Be Loved," and Martina McBride's "Independence Day" and "When God Fearin' Women Get the Blues." She also did a version of the Rascal Flatts's hit "Bless the Broken Road," which prompted phone calls the next day from members of the group who offered their support during her *Idol* competition.

The comments from the judges could be brutal for a young singer, and Underwood soon learned not to enter into any banter back and forth with Simon Cowell, Paula Abdul, or Randy Jackson. Despite Cowell's dislike for country music, he liked the young singer from Oklahoma, commenting that he "looked past" her songs because he felt that she had a likeability factor. In fact, Cowell went so far as to tell the singer that he thought she would win the competition. That comment happened on March 22, after she performed "Alone," a 1987 power ballad by the rock duo Heart. Underwood gave her reasoning for picking this particular song prior to its performance. "Throughout this entire competition I've kind of been a country singer, and I wanted to take a risk and break out of my shell a little bit. So I thought I'd sing an '80s rock song."

Underwood wowed all the judges that night, most of whom had previously expressed appreciation for her voice but not her performances. Randy Jackson told her she was unbelievable and that it was one of her best performances. Paula Abdul said it was a brilliant move and she was proud of her for taking risks. But it was Simon Cowell who surprised everyone, including Underwood. "Carrie, you're not just the girl to beat, you're the person to beat," he told her. "I'll make a prediction: Not only will you win this show; you'll sell more records than any other previous 'Idol' winner." Underwood asked host Ryan Seacrest to pinch her because she didn't believe Cowell had said that. Seacrest did so, telling her, "You're awake. This is real. It's not a dream."[5]

Apparently the viewing audience thought so too. At the time of her involvement with the show, Underwood was only one of three contestants who never entered the bottom three during her weeks of competition. The other two in the category are Kelly Clarkson and Clay Aiken.

Underwood was part of a historic moment on *American Idol* on May 10 when she and Anthony Fedorov both chose the same song to perform. The category for the week was to pick a song from the songwriting team of Kenny Gamble and Leon Huff. Gamble and Huff were two of the writers who contributed to the making of the Philadelphia Sound of the late 1960s and early 1970s. It was pop music with soul, and these two men created much of it through their songwriting and production credits. Before the era was over, they had earned 170 Gold and Platinum records. They formed Philadelphia International Records in 1971 and helped introduce the disco era of music to America. It was the 1972 hit by Harold Melvin & the Blue Notes, "If You Don't Know Me by Now," that attracted the attention of the two contestants.

Underwood told the *Tulsa World* that when a specific category is chosen for a week, contestants get a list of possible songs they can choose from. Occasionally it happens that two people want to do the same song. What made it historic for Underwood and Fedorov was that never before had a male and female chosen the same song to perform on an *Idol* evening. When it was all said and done, the judges liked his version better, but he was voted off the show that night.[6]

While Underwood was competing, her hometown of Checotah and Northeastern State University got behind her wholeheartedly. Local newspapers reminded their readers to watch the show and vote for the hometown favorite. According to the *Tulsa World*, at NSU, Carrie Watch and Voting Parties were held to help encourage fellow students to vote for her.[7] C. H. Parker, who founded the "Downtown Country" show in which Underwood performed while she was at NSU, remembered the singer as "a team player and down-to-earth. She could take the spotlight and sing tremendous solos but also sing harmonies to support her fellow singers."[8] Kelli Doolen, who first met Underwood when she was in high school, told the *Tulsa World* that Underwood had the same voice then that got her into the *American Idol* competition. She said the singer always had an impressive voice, adding "She once sang 'A Broken Wing' by Martina McBride and just blew us away."[9]

When it came down to the final three contestants, Underwood stood strong with Bo Bice and Vonzell Solomon. *American Idol* flew each contestant back to their hometown the Friday after the final three were announced on Wednesday, May 11. As it turned out, Friday the 13th, 2005, would be an awesome day for Underwood. In anticipation that the Oklahoma native would be in that trio, Checotah put together a tremendous welcome for their hometown hero. A crowd that numbered more than 10,000 people stood on rain-drenched streets to watch a parade consisting of fire engines, cars belonging to a racing team from a nearby racetrack, Shriners on horseback, a group of Underwood's fans who worked at Wal-Mart, horseback riders from the Okmulgee Round-Up club, and kids handing out fliers for the Web site carriefans. com. Underwood's ride for the parade was a beautiful horse-drawn carriage, a ride befitting the young college girl who left mid-America to seek stardom in front of millions of television viewers.[10]

Some fans arrived in town before Underwood did, parking their RVs near the television complex where the singer went for interviews before the parade began. Fans were not just proud Oklahomans; folks from surrounding states also drove in to see the possible future *American Idol* winner. A crew from the show was also on hand to capture Underwood's welcome back to her hometown. The *Tulsa World* reported that the number of people at the celebration was three times the population of Chetocah, all with one goal in mind: to offer congratulations and support as they welcomed the singer back to Oklahoma for her big day.

"They kept telling me, 'Oh, it's going to be big, it's going to be big,'" Underwood told the *Tulsa World* during the celebration. "I was like, 'Well, whatever. I've lived there my whole life, you know. Everybody's gonna be cool about it.' So that [number of people] was definitely a shock."[11]

By the time the day was over, Underwood had done numerous interviews and been overloaded with awards, among them the key to the city of Checotah from Mayor Jay Hayes; a "certificate of achievement" from Northeastern State University, from which she would have graduated that month; citations from the Oklahoma Legislature; a Rising Star award from the Oklahoma Music Hall of Fame, and a proclamation of "Carrie Underwood Day" from the governor's office. Underwood was choked with emotion when she told the crowd gathered at Pocket Park after the parade, "You guys mean so much to me."[12]

Organizers of the event heard later that their celebration was the best put together of the three, a huge compliment considering they only had two days to get all the details worked out. In anticipation that Underwood would be in the top three, plans were underway before the announcement on Wednesday, but the actual implementation of those plans didn't begin until the official word was given on *American Idol* that night.

The night the three finalists competed, May 17, 2005, each person sang three songs. Sitting in with the judges was music mogul Clive Davis, who picked the singer's first song for the evening, the Roy Orbison classic "Crying." In general she received good marks for her performance, with Davis saying, "I think you felt the sincerity and strength of the melody." For her second song, Underwood chose the Air Supply number "Making Love out of Nothing at All." Judges Paula Abdul and Randy Jackson thought she did a great job, while Simon Cowell warned that she had pushed the song too much in the middle.[13]

Underwood's third song, Shania Twain's "Man! I Feel Like A Woman!," was chosen for her by Jackson. He sent it to Checotah mayor Jay Hayes, who told Underwood what the selection was at Carrie Underwood Day in her hometown on May 13. Before telling Underwood what song she would be singing, the mayor joked around about the title. "I have with me a facsimile from 'American Idol,' from judge Randy Jackson," he said as he stood before several thousand people in the city's Pocket Park who had turned out for the ceremony. It says, 'I decided that your judge's choice song this week. . . .'" Pausing for effect, he turned to Underwood and said, "It's a great song for you, but Randy, dog, why are you going to make me say this? 'Man! I Feel Like a Woman'—by Shania Twain!"[14]

After she performed the song, Jackson told her, "I'm just happy to see you have some fun up there, man." Davis agreed, telling her he thought country pop was her forte, while Abdul said, "I love it when you're in your element and having fun." Cowell predicted she would make it to the final two, which she did along with Bo Bice.[15]

Going into the final *Idol* competition, Underwood was matter-of-fact about winning or losing. A couple of weeks before she knew she was one of the top two, host Ryan Seacrest asked her about having to be competitive on the show. The singer explained, "This isn't the end of our lives, when the competition's over. So I'm just going to get out here and do the best I can every week, and if I win, YES. But if not, you know, I've still got a life to go home to afterwards."[16]

Fox Network opened an additional phone line for each contestant so fans could get through more easily to vote for their favorites on the next to the last week of *American Idol*. Officials from the network said there had been a higher volume of calls in 2005 than 2004. When the final results were tallied, Underwood and Bice were the two finalists on season four *American Idol*.

As the end of the competition drew near, Underwood looked back on her time with the show and talked about what it was like to be a part of one of the most popular television shows in America. She described it a constant learning experience and told the *Tulsa World* that they were busy all the time. She said once a song has been chosen and performed, each person moves on to the next week and what they have to do to keep on the show. There's not much time for reflection or being a Monday morning quarterback.

"We practice with the band for the first time on Monday. Before that, we practice with our vocal coach, so we know how the song's going to go, but we hear the song with piano and that's it," she told the newspaper. "So we really don't know what it's going to sound like until Monday, and by that time, it's too late to change it. So all you've got to do is suck it up and do the best job you can."[17] Underwood went on to say that when the band starts playing the chosen song, sometimes it sounds like she thought it would and sometimes not.[18]

Once the contestants sing on Tuesday, there's nothing to do but wait and see how the viewing audience votes. Carrie was matter-of-fact about the announcements on Wednesday, when they found out who remained on the show and who was voted off. "If you're still there after Wednesday, obviously it (performance) was OK enough," she pointed out.[19]

Underwood said the contestants are all but cut off from their families and form fast friendships and bonds among each other. There was some speculation that she and Fedorov were a couple after she was caught mouthing "I love you" when he sang his final number on May 10. Underwood quickly put an end to that rumor, saying there was no time among the contestants to have boyfriends or girlfriends.

"Well, when we're with the same people for so long, especially when we're without family and we're without our friends, we have to rely on each other, or we'll go nuts," she told the *Tulsa World*. "Everybody's formed friendships, and Anthony was one of my best friends there. I love him to death. He's like my brother. I mean, he's the most considerate person. He took care of me."[20] However, Underwood went on to say, there was just no time for romance on the set of *Idol*. If they weren't practicing or rehearsing with the band, they were shopping to pick out their clothes for the upcoming show. "They have us under lock and key," she added. "They know where we are at all times, where we are and what we're doing. I mean, everybody pretty much has broken up with their boyfriends or girlfriends. We just don't have time for that."[21]

Underwood did have time to do some television interviews and made one of her most talked-about statements on one of them. When asked if she had seen any "stars" since arriving in California, she replied, "It's been so cloudy, I haven't seen any yet." Underwood might have looked and sounded like a small town girl when she made that statement, but she later said that whenever the *American Idol* crew followed her around, they always seemed to choose the countriest thing she said, or the stupidest thing she did, to air on the show. She felt as if they were trying to make her look more country than she was. In reality, Underwood was a typical college student getting ready to graduate when she entered the *Idol* competition. She was preparing to enter the work force, find a job in her chosen field of journalism, and get on with her life. While *American Idol* took her on a road she had not envisioned, it did allow her to get on with her life in a totally new direction than she had thought it would take.

When it came down to the final night of the fourth season of *American Idol*, which was held at the Kodak Theatre in Hollywood, California, Underwood stood as a semifinalist with Bo Bice, a southern rock singer from Helena, Alabama. The two performed their final songs before an audience of 3,000 fans, including family and friends. The long-haired Bice usually sported bell bottoms and a southern rock attitude that also charmed the judges. They alternately chose Bice and Underwood as their favorites, depending on the song and performance. When the two stood together on the stage that final night, May 25, 2005, Underwood says they had agreed before the show that they would be fine with whoever came out on top.

At one point host Ryan Seacrest asked Underwood what it felt like to be from a small town in Oklahoma and standing in the Nokia theater in Hollywood, California, for the finale of *American Idol*. She replied, "I really don't think I can describe it. This is incredible. Awesome, awesome."[22]

Bice made a risky decision to perform an original song, "The Long, Long Road," which did not please Cowell. The singer redeemed himself with the tune "Inside Your Heaven," which Underwood had also performed at one point in the competition. Underwood chose to perform "Angels Brought Me Here," a pop song written by Jorgen Elofsson and John Reid. Ironically, it was recorded by Guy Sebastian, the 2003 Australian *Idol* winner, for his debut album *Just As I Am* in 2003. He later performed the tune on season four of *American Idol*. After Underwood's performance of the song, Cowell declared he thought she would win the

Carrie Underwood performs during the final performance show of American Idol *at the Kodak Theater in Los Angeles, Tuesday, May 24, 2005. (AP Photo/Kevork Djansezian.)*

competition. The two finalists also performed a duet, singing the pop classic "Up Where We Belong." Both contestants had special moments on the final night of the show. Underwood performed with one of country music's top groups, Rascal Flatts, doing their hit "Bless The Broken Road." Bice sat in with southern rockers Lynyrd Skynyrd.

Throughout the season a record 500 million votes were cast by viewers. When the winner was announced by the show host, Ryan Seacrest, it was Underwood who was declared the "American Idol" for the show's fourth season. She reacted to the announcement by bursting into tears. After gaining her composure, the singer declared it the best night of her life and vowed to remember the moment forever. Nearly 30 million viewers watched the finale of the fourth season of the show.

Once she was named the winner, the business side of the music business kicked in. She was rushed into the studio by 19 Recordings/Arista

Records to record "Inside Your Heaven" and it was immediately released as a single to radio on June 14, 2005. It was her final song to perform for the television studio audience and viewing audience after she was crowned the new "American Idol." In a press release issued by her label, Underwood declared the song's lyrics fitting to her situation, proclaiming "I honestly believe that fate and God [had something to do with the fact] that so many doors opened up the right way for me. My dreams continue to come true," Underwood continued. "Thanks to the fans for voting me as their Idol and for wanting to hear—and have—my music."[23]

Underwood's grandfather, Carl Shatswell, was thrilled for his granddaughter. "I think it's great. She's number one on the radio. I'm going to buy a CD. I never did care much about them CD players, but I will buy one and I'll listen to it somewhere."[24] Others in her hometown of Checotah also bought copies. Janna McKeen bought eight and gave them to friends. Irene Morton, who owns Katy Café, bought six copies, standing in line with Underwood's mother, who was also buying a CD. "I play it here in the restaurant. They just love it," Morton said. "It's probably the most popular song in town. I think everybody in town bought it." Cole Casey, assistant manager at Checotah's Wal-Mart, agreed. He said the store sold 850 copies in one week, with customers averaging 300 copies a week after it had been out for awhile.[25]

Becoming an "American Idol" put Underwood in the company of previous winners Fantasia Barrino, 2004; Ruben Studdard, 2003; and Kelly Clarkson, 2002. She has continued to express her appreciation for the opportunity that being on the show has given her. "I've been very fortunate to have gotten to do a lot of wonderful things. A lot of awards shows and being inducted into the Grand Ole Opry was absolutely definitely one of the highlights of my life. But you know it all started with one amazing journey, and that was 'American Idol'."[26]

She also showed her appreciation to the show by returning numerous times since her win in 2005. The first time she graced its stage after walking away a winner was on March 2, 2006, when she came on the series to perform her hit single, "Jesus, Take the Wheel." She returned on May 24 for the season finale to sing "Don't Forget to Remember Me." The singer returned numerous times over the next few years to perform on the show that gave her a jump start on her career in country music.

Underwood started her professional career by making history in the *Billboard* magazine charts. *Billboard* is the trade magazine that reports on all genres of music. The weekly publication is probably the most-watched magazine in the music industry, as its charts indicate both popularity on radio and sales for the major artists and record labels. "Inside Your Heaven" debuted at the top of *Billboard* magazine's Top 100 the end of June, 2005, marking the first time a country artist debuted at number one on this chart. It also marks the first time a country tune went to number one on that chart since Lonestar's "Amazed" did so in 2000. At the same time, it was number one on the Pop 100, singles sales and country singles sales. "Inside Your Heaven" sold 170,000 copies its first week, giving it the distinction of being the best-selling song of 2005 at that point, according to a press release issued by the record label.

When Underwood made her debut, Tim McGraw had the number one single on the country chart, "Live Like You Were Dyin'." Also in the top 10 were Keith Urban, Toby Keith, Dierks Bentley, George Strait, Sugarland, Kenny Chesney, Faith Hill, Darryl Worley, and Blake Shelton, all entertainers Underwood would be facing when she released her first single to country radio. It was a great lineup of talent, but Underwood ultimately proved that she was up to the task of recording and releasing great country records.

It's interesting also to note that the Oklahoma singer was considered to be a contender in the country market from the very beginning, despite the fact that this first single was not played on country radio. The singer put herself at the heart of country music when she said backstage, "It's been an incredible season for different genres, and hopefully I opened people's eyes to country music."[27] She chose to stay true to country music but left herself open to having some crossover success, as had two of her favorites, Shania Twain and Faith Hill. She was also very gracious when she complimented Bice, saying, "Bo's got an incredible career ahead of him." Bice responded by saying, "You know it's all good. I think America did a great job. I think Carrie fits the bill of an American Idol."[28]

Other celebrities were quick to compliment Underwood on her win. During an event in Denton, Texas on May 31, a fellow Oklahoman commented on the singer's win and ultimate break into country music. "I am very proud of Carrie, and I think she has done a great job," Reba

Carrie Underwood, left, reacts after winning American Idol *as host Ryan Seacrest looks on at the Kodak Theater in Los Angeles, May 25, 2005. Underwood defeated fellow finalist Bo Bice to win. (AP Photo/Kevork Djansezian.)*

McEntire said. "She is as sweet as a button. I think she is going to be a great 'American Idol.'"[29] Although McEntire has homes in Nashville and Los Angeles, she went on to say that Oklahoma is a great place to come back to. "Coming back home grounds you," she said. "It reminds you of your roots and your raising. People from Oklahoma and Texas are just very down to earth people who are loving and giving and supportive."[30]

American Idol's huge fan base supported Underwood by requesting her first single, thus its popularity and consequent number one status on the charts. It became one of the fastest-selling pop singles of all time. Her next single, however, was a 180-degree turn from "Inside Your Heaven" as far as country radio was concerned because it was sent directly to the country market. "Jesus, Take the Wheel" shot up the country charts and made Underwood an instant star to watch in country music.

Underwood signed two endorsement deals with major companies after her *Idol* win. For an artist to endorse a product is immediate money for them, as they are paid to talk about and wear the product, be conspicuous in the product's advertisement campaign, and most likely make appearances at stores where the product is sold as well as do concerts for the company's employees. Underwood signed on with Hershey's chocolate and Skechers shoes, with the latter previously represented by Christina Aguilera and Britney Spears. A year later, on August 11, she became part of the "Got Milk?" campaign when the first advertisement made its debut in USA Today with the tagline "Country by Carrie, Body by Milk."

The endorsements continued in Underwood's career. In April 2008, Glaceau's Vitamin Water signed on to sponsor Underwood's first headline tour. In turn, the singer taped a series of commercials for the vitamin water that began airing in June. "I have a hectic schedule," Underwood said via a press release about the endorsement. "I like to have a lot of energy on stage, and since vitamin water 'Energy' happens to be my favorite flavor, I'm thrilled to have my name on it." Underwood went a step further with the water; she agreed to design a limited-edition bottle label for the bright yellow flavor she likes, Energy, which was available during her "Carnival Ride" tour.

Both finalists received a new red Ford Mustang. Underwood was given the option of the use of a private jet for the year following her win, but she declined the offer, later saying that she would have had to pay the $18,000 in taxes if she took it. She chose to fly first class when she was making trips and representing American Idol. She also received one million dollars and the recording contract. Underwood was 22 years old and the sweetheart of Checotah and music fans across the United States.

While Underwood declared that she wanted her permanent address to be in Oklahoma, she had other things to think about as soon as the final moments of the show were over. In less than two months, Underwood would join the top 10 finalists on the show as they went out on a 40-city "Pop Tarts Presents American Idols Live! Tour 2005." Just as when she was competing on American Idol, Underwood had many days ahead of her preparing for the tour and recording music for her debut album.

The jaunt kicked off in Sunrise, Florida, on July 12 and ended two months later in Syracuse, New York. During the tour the finalists were not only expected to perform, but conduct interviews and generally represent the show in the best light possible. They also promoted their joint CD release, *Showstoppers,* which was released May 21. The CD debuted at number six on *Billboard's* Top 200 chart, selling 81,825 units the first week it was available. In contrast, the 2006 compilation album did not enter into the top 10 of the same *Billboard* chart.

Underwood described time on the road as "rough" but said she learned to be comfortable with the other performers on the tour. Underwood and Bice were joined on the tour by Anthony Federov, Constantine Maroulis, Scott Savol, Vonzell Solomon, Anwar Robinson, Jessica Sierra, Nikko Smith, and Nadia Turner. Audiences heard individual performances from each singer as well as group numbers. They also did tunes from the show's 2004 compilation album *Showstoppers.*

One of the stops on the tour found Underwood performing in Norman, Oklahoma. Governor Brad Henry arranged for the Oklahoma Department of Transportation to place four signs on roads leading into her hometown, which proclaimed "Checotah, Home of Carrie Underwood, American Idol 2005." The governor spoke at a ceremony in Oklahoma City, saying that the signs reflect the pride that Oklahomans have for Carrie. He concluded his remarks by saying, "She is America's Idol, but she was Oklahoma's Idol first." Underwood acknowledged the honor by saying, "As a proud Oklahoman, I'm honored to receive this recognition from my home state and hometown community."

One of the things the singer said about the "American Idol" tour was that it let her, for the first time, connect with those people who had voted for her on the show. She said while the competition was going on, she kept hearing how many people were voting for her, but it was hard for her to comprehend that there were that many people watching the show every week and voting. Once she was on the tour, the people were there in front of her and came up to meet her and get autographs, so she got to see first-hand folks from all age groups who had helped her win the 2005 title.

2005 "American Idol" Tour Dates

- July 12: Sunrise, FL (Office Depot Center)
- July 13: Tampa, FL (St. Pete Times Forum)
- July 15: Birmingham, AL (BJCC Arena)

- July 16: Duluth, GA (The Arena at Gwinnett Center)
- July 17: Greensboro, NC (Greensboro Coliseum)
- July 19: Reading, PA (Sovereign Center)
- July 22: East Rutherford, NJ (Continental Airlines Arena)
- July 23: Uniondale, NY (Nassau Coliseum)
- July 24: Philadelphia, PA (Wachovia Center)
- July 26: Wilkes-Barre, PA (Wachovia Arena)
- July 27: Washington, DC (MCI Center)
- July 29: Hartford, CT (Hartford Civic Center)
- July 30: Worcester, MA (DCU Center)
- July 31: Manchester, NH (Verizon Wireless Arena)
- Aug. 2: Cleveland, OH (Wolstein Center)
- Aug. 3: Columbus, OH (Value City Arena at Schottenstein)
- Aug. 4: Detroit, MI (Joe Louis Arena)
- Aug. 6: St. Paul, MN (Xcel Energy Center)
- Aug. 8: Chicago, IL (United Center)
- Aug. 9: St. Louis, MO (Savvis Center)
- Aug. 12: San Antonio, TX (SBC Center)
- Aug. 13: Grand Prairie, TX (NOKIALive at Grand Prairie)
- Aug. 14: Norman, OK (Lloyd Noble Center)
- Aug. 16: Glendale, AZ (Glendale Arena)
- Aug. 17: Los Angeles, CA (Staples Center)
- Aug. 18: Las Vegas, NV (Thomas & Mack Center)
- Aug. 20: San Jose, CA (HP Pavilion at San Jose)
- Aug. 21: Sacramento, CA (ARCO Arena)
- Aug. 23: Everett, WA (Everett Events Center)
- Aug. 24: Portland, OR (Rose Garden)
- Aug. 26: Salt Lake City, UT (Delta Center)
- Aug. 28: Des Moines, IA (Wells Fargo Arena)
- Aug. 30: Green Bay, WI (Resch Center)
- Aug. 31: Milwaukee, WI (Bradley Center)
- Sept. 2: Albany, NY (Pepsi Arena)
- Sept. 3: Pittsburgh, PA (Mellon Arena)
- Sept. 4: Norfolk, VA (Constant Convocation Center)
- Sept. 8: Providence, RI (Dunkin Donuts Center)
- Sept. 9: Portland, ME (Cumberland County Civic Center)
- Sept. 10: Syracuse, NY (War Memorial at Oncenter)

The final concert of the tour turned out to be a benefit for areas affected by Hurricane Katrina. *American Idol* executive producer Simon Fuller made the suggestion to Underwood and the other *Idol* contestants on the tour and they jumped at the chance to be a part of the hurricane relief effort. Underwood also donated the money made from the sale of her merchandise that evening to the Humane Society of the United States, which was involved in rescuing pets who were separated from their owners in the areas where the hurricane hit.

Reality TV was never a hot topic in Checotah until Underwood became a part of the *American Idol* equation. Suddenly everyone's attention was on the town's new star. During the weeks of competition, Lloyd Jernigan, director of the Chamber of Commerce for the city, told the Associated Press that the singer was probably the number one conversation topic among the town's residents. Those who spoke of her remembered the 22-year-old as polite and quiet with a beautiful voice. Her grandfather says he always thought she'd do something in music because she always loved to sing. He recalled a bus trip with his granddaughter where she wouldn't stop singing. "She went to Kansas one time and was singing on the bus. Her grandmother and me, we tried to get her to hush up, but the rest of the folks on there, they wanted her to keep singing. She was just three at the time."[31]

NOTES

1. Arista Records, Biography, March 2010.

2. Carrie Underwood, American Idol Audition, http://www.youtube.com/watch?v=Mh-8zj5owas, November 29, 2008.

3. Tom Junod, "Carrie Underwood: What I've Learned," http://www.esquire.com/features/what-ive-learned/new-carrie-underwood-interview-0110, December 9, 2009.

4. Peter Cronin, "Carrie Underwood's Wild Ride," CMA News Service, October 4, 2006.

5. John Wooley, "Tracking Checotah's Carrie Underwood in her Quest to Become the Next 'American Idol,' " *Tulsa World*, March 24, 2005.

6. John Wooley, "Carrie On!" *Tulsa World*, May 22, 2005.

7. Matt Gleason, "Carrie Supporters to Watch Their Favorite Idol Show," *Tulsa World*, February 22, 2005.

8. Ibid.

9. Ibid.

10. John Wooley, "Carrie-d Away," *Tulsa World*, May 14, 2005.

11. Ibid.

12. Ibid.

13. Staff reports, "Idol with a Twist," *Tulsa World*, May 19, 2005.

14. Ibid.

15. Ibid.

16. John Wooley, "Carrie On."

17. Ibid.

18. Ibid.

19. Ibid.

20. Ibid.

21. Ibid.

22. Ibid.

23. John Wooley, "Idol Wishes: It's All over Except Tallying Vote," *Tulsa World*, May 25, 2005.

24. Official Blog for West Coast Music In France, http://noted.blogs.com/westcoastmusic/music_charts/, June 26, 2005.

25. "Carrie Underwood Single Tops the Charts," *Tulsa World*, June 24, 2005.

26. Ibid.

27. Ibid.

28. MTV, http://www.mtv.com, March 25, 2005.

29. Ibid.

30. Jay Collington, "Local Star Still a Friend," *Tulsa World*, May 31, 2005.

31. "Carrie Underwood Has Her Town Talking," Associated Press, May 9, 2005.

Stop

Chapter 3

SOME HEARTS

While Underwood was on the 40-city "Pop Tarts Presents American Idols Live! Tour 2005," she was using every spare moment to fly to Nashville to record songs to be included on her first album for 19 Recordings/ Arista Records. The songs that are played on the radio and included on an album can be written by the person singing them, but they can also be penned by songwriters—men and women whose primary career is to write songs for other people to record. Most of these songwriters are represented by publishing companies that pitch the songs to entertainers who are preparing to go in the studio and record.

Singers can find songs to record in several ways. Their producer, manager, and the A&R (Artist & Repertoire) person at the record label all will usually look for songs for them. They contact songwriters that they know personally and ask them to send songs. They also call different publishers who are reputable and they feel sure have great songs and ask them to submit songs for their artist. Often they will seek out songwriters and publishers that they have worked with in the past, because they know the caliber of songs that they have in their catalog (a catalog is the songs at a publishing company or the songs that a songwriter has written).

A person called a song plugger works for each publishing company, and this person keeps up with all the people who are recording. It is their job to pitch songs to artists who are recording. The origin of the term *song plugger* is from the early 20th century, and at that time it referred to a piano player who would play on the mezzanine of a music store in order to help sell sheet music. The store's clientele could ask the pianist to play certain pieces so they could hear what they sounded like before they purchased them. George Gershwin once worked as a song plugger. The term took on its present-day definition later as companies hired people who sought to get songs recorded for their respective publishing companies.

It is very important for the song plugger to have multiple contacts within the music industry. Knowing an artist personally is a great asset; thus many song pluggers like to meet a new artist early in their career, especially if that artist is someone like Underwood who has a built-in fan base from *American Idol*. Often when a bond is established early on between a new singer and a songwriter, publisher, or song plugger, that artist will go back to them time after time, as long as they are being pitched good songs.

If the song plugger does not know the artist, the songs can be sent directly to the producer or manager. Sometimes the song plugger will send them to everyone, thinking that they have a better shot of getting a song heard if more people have the opportunity to hear it. There are also independent song pluggers, who are hired by either the publishing company or the songwriter, to pitch songs. They follow the same procedure as the song plugger at the publishing company—they keep up with who is recording and pitch to the artist, producer, and manager.

Sometimes when an artist is getting ready to record, they will set up meetings with various song pluggers or publishers to listen to songs that are available for them to record. Underwood did not have a history of writing songs at the time she was recording her first album, so this method of finding songs was the path that she chose.

Had Underwood also been a songwriter, she would have turned in a number of songs she had written to the producer. The two would have gone in the studio and recorded 15 or 20 of them, then taken the time to listen to those recordings over a period of several weeks. Finally they would have chosen what they felt were the best 12 songs to go on the album. They could have picked several songs written by other song-writers to include on the CD as well. As it turned out, Underwood had one song that she cowrote on her debut album. Later on she would start to write more songs for her album projects.

Artists who are known as songwriters can write their songs by them-selves, but often they choose to write with established songwriters. When they do, the writers share the songwriting credit and subsequent royal-ties from the songs. There can be any number of people who get to-gether to write a song, but usually there are two or three cowriters on any one song. These people schedule writing appointments and then bring song ideas to the meetings and endeavor to write the best song they can that day.

When an artist is getting ready to record they might come into the meeting with a specific song idea, or they might have a direction they want to go with an album and request that the writers try to write some-thing with a particular feel or sound to it. For instance, if an artist is in the middle of recording they might discover that they have a lot of ballads and mid-tempo songs, but no up-tempo tunes. Then they might come into a writing session and say they need a song that is up-tempo with an upbeat message to it. They could also request a power ballad if they have a lot of up-tempo songs already recorded.

One of country music's mainstays is the story song. Occasionally an artist will come in with a story about something that happened to them or a friend, describe the situation, and then they and their cowriters will sit down and write a song about it. This personalizes the album for the artist and gives fans a chance to get to know about them through their tunes. A classic example of artists recording songs about their life is George Jones and Tammy Wynette, who practically laid out their life for their fans in the songs they recorded. Loretta Lynn was also known for writing songs that depicted what she was going through in her life at the time she recorded them. Another example among Underwood's peers is Taylor Swift, who writes quite a few songs about ex-boyfriends who didn't treat her right.

While Carrie had been in a recording studio before her first record-ing session in Nashville, those endeavors had not been as intense as the ones she would do for her first major album release. Her career was literally on the line as she went in to record her freshman album. She knew if that record didn't sell, and the songs that were sent to country radio didn't get played, she would more than likely lose her record deal after the contract ran out. This put a lot of pressure on Underwood as she went through the process of choosing songs and recording.

When it came to choosing songs, Underwood was able to get tunes from some of the top writers in the business. Early in the process of picking songs, she was introduced to hit writers like Hillary Lindsey, Brett James, and Rivers Rutherford, who also agreed to write with the young artist. Since Underwood was so new to Nashville, it was a good idea for her management to put her with the writers who would shape the direction of her debut disc. The group of writers, along with the singer, got together at Nashville's Karian Studios. The opportunity to meet and talk with each other was invaluable in giving the writers a look into the person they would be pitching songs to. It also gave Underwood a chance to rub shoulders with some of the best songwriters in Nashville, and it made her even more determined that she would hone her craft in order to make a place for her among their ranks.

"I wanted to meet the songwriters, get to know them and let them know the kind of album I wanted to make," Underwood told CMA *Close Up*. "They broke off into little groups and I'd bounce around from room to room and give suggestions and sing part of what they'd written. We even recorded some rough drafts right there in the studio. 'I Ain't in Checotah Anymore' came from that time, and I co-wrote on another one that didn't make the album. I can't wait to get into the next one. I want to have a bigger hand in it and co-write on a lot more songs."[1]

Meeting and getting to know these songwriters did something else for Underwood—it helped her break the stigma a new artist might have when they arrive in Nashville as a total unknown. When that happens, the major writers won't give them their songs because they don't know if they will have a hit with their first album release. Admittedly it was somewhat different with Underwood because of the *American Idol* connection. With the proven success of previous *Idol* winners like Kelly Clarkson, it seemed more likely that Underwood would have hits right away. Bearing that information in mind, Nashville hit tunesmiths Lindsey, James, Rutherford, Troy Verges, Trey Bruce, and others including pop writer Diane Warren contributed tunes for Underwood to record.

Most studios today have at least 24-track recording capabilities and record digitally instead of to tape. Some of the bigger studios have 48-track recording capability or more. Underwood would rely on her producer and record label to choose a studio and the musicians who would play on the album. There can be any number of musicians on one of Carrie's projects, depending on the kind of song she is recording. Basically there would be a lead guitar, rhythm guitar, piano, drums, and bass guitar. Many country songs include a mandolin, fiddle, steel guitar, or banjo, as well as any other instruments the producer thinks will add to the emotion and feel of the tune.

The producer on a recording project is the person who directs the entire album. The label chose to put her with two producers who had track records with major artists. Dann Huff, who has worked with Keith Urban, Faith Hill, and the group Lonestar, and Mark Bright, whose roster of clients includes Rascal Flatts, Jo Dee Messina, and Sara Evans, guided the recording on Underwood's debut album.

Many producers today are more hands-on instead of just overseeing the recording sessions. They do everything to ensure the session comes off for the artist. They oversee the recording and work with the recording engineer to get the sound right and ensure the artist's voice sounds the best it can possibly sound. They often have favorite musicians, studios, and engineers that they call to work the sessions.

The engineer works behind the board, which controls all the instruments that are on the session as well as the vocals. It is the engineer's responsibility to make sure that each instrument is balanced with all other instruments, and that the singer's vocals are out in front of the band so people can hear the words to the songs as well as the music.

Once the songs have been recorded, the engineer mixes them to give each tune the best quality it can have. This is done by balancing the music to make sure that all the vocals as well as the musical instruments sound harmonious. In country music the artist's voice is usually mixed in front of the instruments, so that listeners can easily hear the lyrics to the song. Much of country music is story songs, so it is important that all the words are audible to the person listening to the record.

After the songs are mixed the entire album is sent to be mastered. The mastering engineer has an entirely different job from the mixing engineer. This person's job is to ensure that the album as a whole has the same level, so that the listener doesn't have to constantly change the volume as each songs plays. There are standards the mastering engineer goes by as they add or subtract levels to give the project a cohesive feel and sound. The reason this is necessary is that an artist will probably record an album over several days, maybe in two or three different studios with different musicians. One day the drummer may be playing louder than the previous day, or the artist's vocals might be more powerful than they have been. Whatever the case, the mastering engineer can make it all sound as if it were recorded in one take, all at one level. This doesn't change anything the mixing engineer and producer have done in previous sessions; it just enhances it and ensures better listening quality for the person who buys the music.

Once the mastering engineer completes their work, the master tape is sent on to the pressing plant, where CDs are manufactured for retail sales. It is at this plant that the booklets that often accompany a CD are printed and put together with the disc inside the plastic packaging. Then the CD is shipped off to various retail outlets around the country where consumers can buy them.

Songs from the album are also offered by online sites—iTunes, Amazon, and Wal-Mart are all huge online outlets where fans can purchase individual songs or the entire album. They take the songs after the mastering engineer is finished with them and place them on their sites for purchase by the consumer. Once the fans have the opportunity to buy the CDs or download the songs, the artist finds out how the public likes the music that they have recorded.

Before Underwood's album was released for sale, the record label released a second single, "Jesus, Take the Wheel." Underwood described the song as a very touching story about asking for help and went on to say that it is something most people can identify with, because there comes a time in everyone's life when they realize they cannot control everything going on in their life. Underwood performed it on the Country Music Association's awards show November, 15, 2005, which originated from New York City for the first and only time. It was the first single released to country radio, and the song raced to the top of the country charts after entering Billboard's country singles chart at number 39. It stayed at number one for six weeks, immediately earning Underwood the distinction of being one of the country female vocalists able to claim that honor. She and Faith Hill, Taylor Swift, and Kitty Wells have all had songs at the top of the charts for six weeks. Only Connie Smith, with her tune "Once a Day," has held down the number one position for a longer period of time. The song went on to be a crossover hit—a single that charts in more than one musical genre—climbing to number 20 on *Billboard*'s Hot 100 chart.

The debut album was released in November 2005. Prior to its release, not only had Underwood been on the "American Idol" tour, she had the opportunity to appear in front of thousands of country music fans at other events. In June, just after her win, the singer performed at the annual CMA Music Festival in Nashville. More than 50,000 fans come to Nashville for the festival, and Underwood found it exciting to be able to perform on several of its stages, including the main one at the Nashville arena. She remembers having a very warm reception from everyone in Nashville, fans and music industry people as well.

"I'd been to Nashville to attend Fan Fair (what the festival was originally called) before, but I was on the other side," Underwood remembers. "I got to meet a lot of fans, and that was great to be able to put faces with people who had followed me on 'American Idol' and maybe voted for me."[2] One of the reasons Underwood was so insistent on being at the CMA Music Festival so soon after her *American Idol* win was that she wanted to establish early in her career that she intended to make her career in country music. She declared that she liked all genres of music, but being from Oklahoma, country music was a natural choice for her.

"We'd take car trips and my parents always had it on the oldies station," she told CMA *Close-up* about her background in music." I got a lot of Rolling Stones, Creedence Clearwater Revival, John Denver, and all that. My sisters were teenagers when I was growing up and they were in their rebellious stage, so I got a lot of '80s rock music out of them. But being from Oklahoma, country music was always playing everywhere. In every store you went into, if there was a radio on, 95-percent of the time it was a country station. So it was something that had a lot of influence on me. I love all kinds of music, but I feel like I fit with country and that's the kind of music I love."[3]

While in Nashville to perform at CMA Music Fest, Underwood was called upon to tape CMT's (Country Music Television) "100 Greatest

Duets." She sang the Reba McEntire/Linda Davis hit, "Does He Love You," with Jamie O'Neal for the special. "I knew the words so it was okay [to do that song]," Underwood said at the time. "It was a hit for Reba and Linda, so it was a cool song to get to do."[4] It was also a night for her to meet some of her country music heroes, as the talent line-up for the taping read like a who's who in country music: Trace Adkins, Keith Anderson, Clint Black, Terri Clark, Miranda Lambert, Montgomery Gentry, Joe Nichols, Dolly Parton, Kenny Rogers, Blake Shelton, and Marty Stuart were just a few of the stars on hand for the occasion.

On June 10, 2005, Underwood made her *Grand Ole Opry* debut, just two weeks after winning *American Idol*. She was introduced by Country Music Hall of Famer and Grand Ole Opry member Bill Anderson, and she performed the Roy Orbison classic "Crying." Many country singers wait years before they are invited to make an *Opry* appearance. Like most other country singers, Underwood admits that she was a fan of the *Opry* when she was growing up and watched it on television as well as listened to it on the radio on Friday and Saturday night, dreaming of one day performing on the world-famous show. She even dared to dream that one day she might become a member of the Grand Ole Opry family.

For country entertainers and fans, the Grand Ole Opry is a mecca for country music. The *Opry* began as the WSM *Barn Dance* on November 28, 1925, when George D. Hay, known as The Solemn Old Judge, harmonica player DeFord Bailey, and fiddler Uncle Jimmy Thompson kicked off what would become the longest running radio show in America. The show was renamed the *Grand Ole Opry* in 1927, allegedly when it came on after an opera performance. Legend has it that Hay came on the air after Bailey's first song and announced "For the past hour, we have been listening to music taken largely from Grand Opera. From now on we will present the Grand Ole Opry." The name was an instant success.

In 1932, when WSM Radio became a 50,000 watt station, much of the United States and a good part of Canada could hear the show, resulting in more and more people coming to Nashville to see its weekend performances. The Opry changed homes several times, arriving at the Ryman Auditorium in 1943. It is now called "The Mother Church of Country Music," because the venue was originally built by Captain Thomas Ryman for evangelist Samuel Jones as a church where Jones would hold his revivals. The show became so popular that tickets sold out in advance, and there are many photos of people lined up around the building on Fifth Avenue North and down Broadway, waiting for the doors to open and the show to begin.

The Opry remained at the Ryman until 1974, when the brand new Grand Ole Opry House was built on the grounds of Opryland U.S.A., an amusement park and recreation center along the Cumberland River about 15 miles away from downtown Nashville. Today the majority of the *Opry* performances are there, but in the winter months the show returns to the Ryman for performances November through January. The amusement park is long gone, and a huge mall has replaced the rides, shows, and concession stands.

Underwood also had the opportunity to perform on the 39th annual CMA Awards show on November 15, 2005, when the CBS-TV special was held in New York City for the first time. That same day her debut album, *Some Hearts,* was released. She told AP, "Instead of going through it all twice, this mashed everything together." Backstage she admitted, "I went to a record store this morning and bought my album. . . . It's been surreal."[5]

Performing on the CMA show in New York was a great debut for Underwood, who sang "Jesus, Take the Wheel" for the television audience. Also on the show was fellow Oklahoman Garth Brooks, who performed his new single, "Good Ride, Cowboy" from Times Square. Also making appearances were Sugarland's Jennifer Nettles with Bon Jovi, Keith Urban, Rascal Flatts, George Strait, Gretchen Wilson, and Lee Ann Womack. Hosts for the event were Brooks & Dunn, which included another Oklahoman, Ronnie Dunn.

Winning *American Idol* and her consequent success as a recording artist afforded Underwood many more opportunities than she had ever dreamed of. On June 16, 2005, Underwood was asked to sing the national anthem before game four of the National Basketball Association's finals at the Palace of Auburn Hills, in Michigan, when the Detroit Pistons won over the San Antonio Spurs, 102–71. It was a natural for her to perform at a sports event, because Underwood is an admitted sports fan. She would go on to perform the National Anthem at many other sporting events in the next few years, including the NFC championship game between the Seattle Seahawks and the Carolina Panthers on January 22, 2006. When Underwood was given a pair of tickets to Super Bowl XL after performing at the NFC game, she gave them to her sister and brother-in-law, because prior commitments made it impossible for her to make use of them. While the singer said she would usually have been thrilled to go to the Super Bowl, she was happy to be able to pass the tickets along to her family so they could go and enjoy the game and surrounding festivities. Only a month later she found herself performing at halftime of the NBA All-Star Game in Houston, Texas. On May 28, 2006, Underwood performed at a different sporting event, NASCAR's Coca-Cola 600 at Lowe's Motor Speedway in Concord, North Carolina. She also performed the National Anthem at the 77th Major League Baseball All-Star Game at PNC Park in Pittsburgh, Pennsylvania, on July 11, 2006.

Country singer Carrie Underwood performs the National Anthem before the start of the NFL Super Bowl XLIV football game between the Indianapolis Colts and New Orleans Saints in Miami, Feb. 7, 2010. (AP Photo/David J. Phillip.)

Underwood's appearances to a mass audience through *American Idol* and her introduction to the music industry and the fans set the stage for her to be thrust into the limelight more quickly than any other country artist at that time. Her debut album and consequent singles reflected that in sales and radio airplay.

NOTES

1. Peter Cronin, "Carrie Underwood's Wild Ride," CMA *Close-Up*, October 24, 2006.

2. Pam Green, Carrie Underwood Interview, Westwood One Radio Network, November 12, 2008.

3. Cronin, "Carrie Underwood's Wild Ride."

4. Ibid.

5. Jake Coyle, "Underwood Talks about Debut Disc, Awards Show," Associated Press release, November 17, 2005.

Chapter 4

JESUS, TAKE THE WHEEL

Before Underwood released "Jesus, Take the Wheel," the record label took her on what is called a promo tour, visiting radio stations to introduce her to the deejays who would be playing her song. When a new artist is going out to meet radio, a representative who is a member of the label's promotion team will go with them to make the introductions and see that the artist meets the right people at the station.

It is not possible for an artist to go to all the country radio stations in the United States since there are nearly 2,000 stations that play country music. The label rep generally takes the new artist to the major stations that make up the *Billboard* singles charts. There are 125 stations that are monitored each week to see what music they play. These stations are in major and medium markets around the United States and include cities ranging from Los Angeles to Charleston, West Virginia, according to *Billboard* chart editor Wade Jessen. Broadcast Data System, a subsidiary of *Billboard*, monitors the stations, and a list is compiled of the top 75 songs in the United States according to *Billboard*.

To help get the song played on radio, the record label has a promotion team of people who call radio stations daily to see if they have received the new record and if they are playing it or intend to play it.

A few of the people are actually at the label office in Nashville; many of them live in the area they represent, such as Houston or Atlanta for the Southeast, Los Angeles for the West Coast area, or Chicago for the Mid-America states. These men and women know the deejays, program directors, and music directors personally and can work with them to encourage them to play the record that they are trying to get played at the time.

Program directors are the men and women who decide what records will be played on country radio. Occasionally there is another person involved in that decision-making process, called a consultant, who takes polls of what the country fan wants to hear and advises stations accordingly. The songs that a station is playing make up a play list. On rare occasion, the deejay is allowed to make up his or her play list. This happened a lot when radio was young, but it is a rare thing these days for deejays to have liberty to play what he they want to play on his their show.

Sometimes a new artist has difficulty getting their records played on radio because the listeners at radio stations don't know who they are. Underwood didn't have too much trouble in that respect, because radio station personnel already knew her from *American Idol*. When "Jesus, Take the Wheel" arrived on their desks, the record promoters were able to persuade them to play it without much convincing, because program directors knew their listeners probably watched *Idol* and knew that Underwood had just won the competition in 2005.

The next stage of a career after a singer starts to have their record played on radio is for them to be booked on a major concert tour so they can perform in front of their fans. Although Underwood had been a performer on the "Pop Tarts Presents American Idols Live! Tour 2005," she had not been presented to the country music audience specifically.

To book a tour a singer needs a booking agency. The singer signed with Creative Artists Agency (CAA), with offices in Nashville and other major cities around the world. The company is one of the largest booking agencies in the world. This is good for a new artist like Underwood, who needs to be in front of as many people as possible, as fast as possible, to increase record sales and boost her own visibility level so one day she can go out on a headline tour of her own.

A booking agent not only places their clients on concert tours; if they have the right connections, they can get them on major television shows and into made-for-TV movies and also major motion pictures. If the need is there, they can also land them major book deals and other things that will help further their career. While Underwood was not ready for most of these things that first year, it was important to be with an agency like CAA, because they could certainly handle deals like that for her as her career progressed.

Sometimes an agency will put a new artist like Underwood on tour with one of their other artists in the same genre; other times they will place them on a tour where they think their client will get the maximum exposure. In the case of Underwood, the first thing they did was put her out on the fair and festival circuit, where she could perform in front of major groups of country music fans. She was scheduled to do 40 solo performances, the majority of them during the peak of the season for outdoor events, late spring through early fall. Later during that same timeframe, she joined Kenny Chesney's "The Road and the Radio" tour for 20 dates between June 1 and Labor Day, 2006. "I saw Kenny in concert when I was 16 years old and it's now a dream come true to be going on tour with him," Underwood said through her publicist via a press release. "As a record label mate, he has been very encouraging since my album came out and I have great admiration for him for all he's done in his career," she added.[1]

Chesney was already huge at this time, with his tour selling out every night to 20,000-plus audiences. *Pollstar,* the major magazine for concert tours, cited Chesney as the most successful country touring act of 2005, grossing $61.8 million in 71 shows. It was a great move for Underwood, who really had no previous history performing in front of such large numbers of fans, to be able to join his tour. Dierks Bentley filled the bill as the lead-in to Chesney, and Underwood was billed as the opening act.

"I knew we were gonna need to come up with something pretty special," Chesney said in a press release issued by his publicist. "Dierks actually had that opening slot, so he's a natural as he's coming into his own to be out here with us . . . and when we started looking around for someone who all the people who've been coming to see us, who have some pretty high expectations, we knew we needed someone who'd really stand out. Needless to say, I think Carrie Underwood's the real deal . . . and I'm psyched she's gonna be on the road with us."[2]

"It is so thrilling to be able to get back out and perform for the fans again," Underwood said through her publicist via a press release. "We put a band together last year to launch the album with radio and television promotion. We are all itching to get on a bus and really travel across the states and see the real America."[3]

By the time Underwood was on the concert trail, her debut album, *Some Hearts*, had sold two million copies. The fans were willing to put their money down for her album, so it was a good bet that they were willing to pay their money to see her perform. It was a win/win situation for her and her touring partner—she would be singing in front of thousands of fans, and Chesney would sell a few tickets to someone who might otherwise not have come to his concert if the *American Idol* winner had not been on it.

Underwood was part of several very special moments while on the Chesney tour. She joined the entertainer and Dierks Bentley for a sold-out show at Madison Square Garden in New York City on July 14, 2006. Two days later, Chesney, along with Bentley, Underwood, Gretchen Wilson, and Big & Rich, set a new record for a country music show at Gillette Stadium in Foxboro, Massachusetts, just outside of Boston. The show was a sell-out in the 50,000-seat stadium.

Underwood did very well on this tour, and by the time it ended she was booked to head out with another top star, Brad Paisley. Paisley and Underwood both record for Arista Records; Chesney records for a different label, BNA, under the same parent company as Arista, RCA. So in reality, Chesney and Paisley were extending a helping hand to a fellow labelmate, much as singers had done for both of them when they first started out.

Underwood had a short break between the end of the Chesney tour and the beginning of Paisley's "Time Well Wasted" tour. She took advantage of those days to do another leg of shows at state fairs. She kicked off Paisley's tour on September 22 in Birmingham, Alabama, and closed it out with him on December 8 in Chicago, Illinois. Joining them on the tour was country rocker Eric Church. The combination of talent was a good one for fans, as the show included several elements of country music for one ticket price.

Reviews for Underwood were positive during her these early concert tours. Concertlivewire.com caught the singer in Twin Lakes, Michigan, for the Country Thunder Festival. Reporter Robin Mayer said Underwood has "a fine strong voice that translates well in either country or rock." The reporter did say that Underwood was still "new to the business of performing" and "a little uncomfortable with the banter that goes with a live performance." Mayer described Underwood's show as having a few surprises. Along with songs from her debut album she also included songs from rockers Guns 'n Roses and Aerosmith.[4]

The Syracuse, New York *Post-Standard* reported on her performance at the New York State Fair, saying she was more comfortable onstage than her previous appearance there during the "American Idol" tour in 2005, even dancing around the stage as she sang. In September, a reviewer for the *American Idol* Web site caught Underwood in Ridgewood, Washington, at the Clark County Amphitheatre. The writer observed that the singer's stage presence had improved and "she seems much more comfortable with her superstardom and popularity."[5]

While Underwood was busy on tour in 2006, she also took part in a very special recording. *Oklahoma Rising,* a double CD celebrating Oklahoma's Centennial, was released on September 22 by the Oklahoma Centennial Commission. The set features 46 songs by 43 Oklahoma artists and groups, giving an overview of the state's musical history. In addition to Underwood, the discs feature artists Vince Gill, Sandi Patti, Brooks & Dunn, Reba McEntire, the Tractors, the Flaming Lips, Garth Brooks, the All-American Rejects, Toby Keith, and singer/songwriter Jimmy Webb.

By the end of 2006, Underwood had done over 150 shows, ending the year by headlining a USO tour during the Christmas holiday season, performing for U.S. troops in Kuwait and Iraq.

The "Road and the Radio" Tour with Kenny Chesney's Dierks Bentley and Carrie Underwood (* Indicates Carrie as Opening Act)

June 1   Evansville, IN (Roberts Stadium)

June 2   Grand Rapids, MI (Van Andel Arena)*

June 3   Grand Rapids, MI (Van Andel Arena)*

June 4   Fort Wayne, IN (Allen County Memorial Coliseum)*

June 13   Oakland, CA (Oakland Arena)*

June 15   Glendale, AZ (Glendale Arena)*

June 16   Las Vegas, NV (Mandalay Bay Events Center)*

June 17   Carson, CA (Home Depot Center)*

June 18   Chula Vista, CA (Coors Amphitheatre)*

June 21   Salt Lake City, UT (Usana Amphitheatre)*

June 24   Seattle, WA (Qwest Field)

July 1   Tampa, FL (Raymond James Stadium)

July 4   Milwaukee, WI (Marcus Amphitheater)*

July 8   Nashville, TN (The Coliseum)*

July 11   Calgary, AB Canada (Pengrowth Saddledome)

July 14   New York, NY (Madison Square Garden)

July 16   Foxboro, MA (Gillette Stadium)

July 27   Hartford, CT (New England Dodge Music Center)*

July 28   Bristow, VA (Nissan Pavilion)*

July 30   Burgettstown, PA (Post Gazette Pavilion at Star Lake)*

Aug. 10   Charlotte, NC (Verizon Wireless Amphitheatre)*

Aug. 11   Raleigh, NC (Alltel Pavilion)*

Aug. 13   Virginia Beach, VA (Verizon Wireless Amphitheatre)*

Aug. 26   Detroit, MI (Ford Field)

Aug. 30   Charlottesville, VA (John Paul Jones Arena)*

Sept. 1   St. Louis, MO (Savvis Center)*

Sept. 2   Chicago, IL (Bridgeview Stadium)

Sept. 3   Noblesville, IN (Verizon Wireless Music Center)*

**"Time Well Wasted" Tour with Brad Paisley,
Eric Church, and Carrie Underwood**

Sept. 22   Birmingham, AL (Verizon Wireless Music Center)

Sept. 23   Atlanta, GA (Phillips Arena)

Sept. 24   Pensacola, FL (Pensacola Civic Center)

Sept. 28   Holmdel, NJ (PNC Bank Arts Center)

Sept. 29   Columbus, OH (Germain Amphitheater)

Sept. 30   Cincinnati, OH (Riverbend Music Center)

Oct. 19   Peoria, IL (Peoria Civic Center Arena)

Oct. 20   Ft. Wayne, IN (War Memorial Coliseum)

Oct. 21   Cape Girardeau, MO (Show Me Center)

Oct. 26   Trenton, NJ (Sovereign Bank Arena)

Oct. 27   Verona, NY (Turning Stone Resort & Casino)

Oct. 28   Baltimore, MD (First Mariner Center)

Nov. 2   Jackson, MS (Mississippi Coliseum)

Nov. 3   Lafayette, LA (Cajundome)

Nov. 4   Houston, TX (Cynthia Woods-Mitchell Pavilion-Woodlands)

Nov. 9   Columbia, SC (Colonial Center)

Nov. 10   Greenville, SC (Bi-Lo Center)

Nov. 11   Savannah, GA (Savannah Convention Center)

Nov. 16   San Antonio, TX (AT&T Center)

Nov. 17   Wichita Falls, TX (Kay Yeager Coliseum)

Nov. 18   Oklahoma City, OK (Ford Center)

Nov. 30   Colorado Springs, CO (World Arena)

Dec. 1   Salt Lake City, UT (Delta Center)

Dec. 2   Las Vegas, NV (Mandalay Bay Events Center)

Dec. 7   Columbia, MO (Mizzou Arena)

Dec. 8   Chicago, IL (Allstate Arena)

NOTES

1. Press Release, Schmidt Public Relations, March 3, 2006.

2. Academy of Country Music Web site, March 15, 2006, http://www.acountry.com.

3. Press Release, Schmidt Public Relations, March 3, 2006.

4. Robin Mayer, "Country Has a Home in the North," http://www.concertlivewire.com/country06.htm, July 23, 2006.

5. "American Idol Worship Exclusive: Review of Carrie Underwood Concert in Clark County, Washington," September 26, 2006, http://www.americanidol.com.

Chapter 5

CHANGE

When Underwood set out to record her first album that would be released nationally, it was an entirely new process for her. Certainly she had been in the studio before, but only to record for her own pleasure and for the possibility of someone hearing it who might offer her a recording contract. This time, the recording she made could literally make or break her career.

Underwood had much to learn about the music business. Although she had always loved to sing, there is a vast difference from loving to sing, and singing in the local church or civic group, to setting out to make singing a career. Checotah, Oklahoma, did not offer much in the way of an education for a young woman who thought she might want to be a singer of national and/or international reputation. She could read books, take singing lessons, and read stories in entertainment trade magazines like *Billboard* or *Variety*, but there were no local colleges that offered a degree in "Country Singing 101."

One of the intriguing things about a career in the arts is there is no guarantee that a person is going to make it in their chosen profession. An individual who goes to college and gets a degree as a lawyer, computer technician, nurse, or doctor can hope to graduate and get a job. A person who wants to be a singer, no matter what genre they choose, does not know if they will ever make it because there are so many variables. Being a talented singer, or even an amazing singer, is not the sole requirement. Meeting the right person, that is, a record producer or record company executive, always helps. Moving to a music center, such as Nashville, Los Angeles, New York, Atlanta, or Detroit, is a valuable consideration. Meeting a songwriter, publisher, or any other music executive in that city, and having them like what the singer does, will help. In more recent years, performing on *American Idol* and lasting through enough episodes so that the contestant gains a fan following and a record company executive, producer, or publisher recognizes them is a great way to land that recording deal and get a shot at stardom.

With Underwood winning *American Idol,* she had a much better chance than many of the contestants who were on the same season with her, but there was still no guarantee. If she didn't choose the songs that radio would play or that the fans who voted for her on *Idol* would like, or if she became a diva and decided that she was already a star because she was the winner, she might not get that first album released.

Underwood was fortunate in that she had a level head on her shoulders, she had an idea of the direction she wanted to take her career, and she ended up with a good team of people around her who helped guide her career in that first year when she was really becoming a presence in music. While she could have chosen to be a pop star, the Oklahoman felt that she needed to tackle the country music market. Everything about her background indicated country with a pop leaning, which was very prevalent when she entered the country music market in 2005.

Immediately after winning *American Idol,* Underwood's first single, "Inside Your Heaven," written by Andreas Carlsson, Pelle Nylen, and Savan Kotecha, was released. The tune debuted at number one on *Billboard*'s Hot 100 chart, selling 170,000 the first week it was released. It was the first song from a country singer to achieve that chart position since the group Lonestar went number one with their hit song "Amazed" in 2000. "Inside Your Heaven" also debuted at number one on *Billboard*'s Pop 100 Singles Sales chart and Country Singles Sales chart. It was certified Gold by the Recording Industry Association of America (RIAA) on July 26, 2005. The song made digital Gold on November 18, 2005.

Underwood's second single set several records in country music after it was released. The single, "Jesus, Take The Wheel," penned by Nashville songwriters Brett James, Hillary Lindsey, and Gordie Sampson, was released October 18, 2005. The song stayed at number one for six weeks and became the first single by a new artist to debut inside the Top 40 on the country charts since the inception of the Broadcast Data System (BDS) in 1990. BDS is the system that tracks songs that are played on the radio and the system by which *Billboard* determines its singles charts. "Jesus, Take the Wheel" was certified a Gold single on December 11, 2005, and Platinum on July 30, 2008. It also became a Gold digital single on January 25, 2006 and a Gold Mastertone single on December 11, 2006. The certification for Mastertone singles out ring tones for cell phones.

Underwood experienced another first when "Jesus, Take the Wheel" was released. On October 20, 2005, the singer shot her first video. She did the shoot for "Jesus, Take the Wheel" in Nashville with director Roman White, who would work with her on many of her future video productions as well. It went on to be named CMT's Breakthrough Video of the Year for 2005, as well as the network's Female Video of the Year. It stayed at the top of CMT's Top Twenty Countdown for three weeks. In December 2006 Underwood found out that her first video was number five in CMT's Top 20 Video Countdown for 2006. It also came in at 64 on the network's 100 Greatest Videos. It was also played on Christian video outlets.

Underwood performed in her first major network Christmas show in the fall of 2005. She was asked to sing in the NBC special, "Christmas in Rockefeller Center," on November 30. She joined Sheryl Crow, Brian Wilson, Rod Stewart, Earth, Wind & Fire, and Regis Philbin for the annual event. A week later she performed a Country Cares Concert for hurricane relief at the Palace of Auburn Hills near Detroit, Michigan. This was a great introduction for Carrie, as she learned that country singers really do care, and they can often be seen participating in benefits for various causes. Also on the show were Martina McBride and LeAnn Rimes. Later in the month she joined Rascal Flatts, gospel great CeCe Winans, Ciara and the Click Five, performing for President George W. Bush at the National Building Museum in Washington, D.C. The concert turned into a Christmas special for TNT titled "Christmas in Washington," which aired on December 14, 2005.

Underwood had an interesting third single release. The label sent the title cut from the album, *Some Hearts*, to pop, adult contemporary, and hot adult contemporary radio stations in October 2005. The tune climbed into the top 25 on the Hot AC chart and into the top 15 on the AC Chart. "Some Hearts" also had the distinction of being performed by Underwood on a float in front of a huge inflatable jukebox in the 2005 Macy's Thanksgiving Day Parade.

The label then released "Don't Forget to Remember Me," cowritten by Morgane Hayes, Kelley Lovelace, and Ashley Gorley, all Nashville-based songwriters, to country radio, in March 2006. This was Underwood's third single to country radio. It went to number one on the Radio & Records Country Chart and number two on *Billboard*'s Hot Country Songs chart. It also climbed to number 49 on the magazine's Hot 100.

The video for "Don't Forget to Remember Me" was a special one for Underwood. The song is about a young girl leaving home, asking that the people she is leaving behind not forget her. The story touched the singer's heart because when she first heard it, she knew she would be going through similar experiences as the narrator in the song. Her mother felt the same way when she heard it the first time.

Carole Underwood said that as *American Idol* came to an end her daughter was listening to songs that were being sent to her. One day she saw a lyric that Carrie had left on the table and when she read it, it deeply affected her. "It choked me up, it was just real touching," Mrs. Underwood told Westwood One. "Then when they were going to do a video I told Carrie that I could play the part of the mom. She said, 'Mother, they'll hire somebody to do that.'" "Then a couple weeks later she called me and said, 'You know, they, uh, I was told to call you and see if you might like to be the mother in my video.' I laughed and said 'Yes I think I can do that.' She said there would be some acting involved but I thought that surely I could play her mother!"[1] The video was shot in Nashville, so Mrs. Underwood flew in and did a great job at portraying herself. "Don't Forget to Remember Me" debuted on CMT on March 16, 2006.

On March 2, 2006, Underwood returned to the stage of *American Idol,* this time as a performer. She sang her country hit "Jesus, Take the Wheel" and noted it was good to be back but not have to worry about being judged for her performance! She also said it was good to be asked to be back on the show as a performer and added that she hoped to share some tips and advice with the season five contestants.

A month later, on April 10, 2006, Underwood attended the CMT Video Awards. She had landed three nominations, among them Breakthrough Video, Female Video, and Most Inspiring Video for "Jesus, Take the Wheel." By the end of the night, the singer had two trophies for her soon-to-be built trophy case, Breakthrough Video and Female Video. Underwood also had her first bit of controversy at these awards. Backstage in the press room, Wynonna Judd was asked what she thought of the singer. She admitted that she did not know a lot about Underwood but thought she was a good singer. Judd then launched into her opinion of new country singers, calling them vanilla and wishing for a little more soul from them. Underwood was standing in the wings and heard her comment. Underwood came out immediately after Judd left the stage, but in the midst of her time with the press, Judd returned to clarify that she was not talking about Underwood, but about the music in general, when she made those statements. Nevertheless, the media talked about the incident for days, even after Underwood said she never thought Judd was talking about her.

On May 23, 2006, Underwood attended the 41st annual Academy of Country Music Awards in Las Vegas, Nevada. She had garnered three awards nominations—Top New Female Vocalist, Top Female Vocalist, and Single Record for "Jesus, Take the Wheel." Underwood and the song's writers, Brett James, Hillary Lindsey, and Gordon Sampson, also received a nod for Song of the Year honors. Underwood added more trophies to her case, taking home Top New Female Vocalist and Single of the Year honors. Underwood also performed two songs during the telecast, the hit single, "Jesus, Take the Wheel," and her upcoming single, "Before He Cheats." The show aired live from the MGM Grand in Las Vegas.

Underwood returned home to perform her first major concert since becoming a national recording act on June 8, 2006. She performed at Pryor, Oklahoma's Country Fever festival, closing the opening night festivities after fellow Oklahoman Wade Hayes. Underwood had many fans in the audience who had watcher her, and cheered her on, during her *American Idol* days. She told the audience that she appreciated the opportunity of winning the talent contest and getting to do all she has done in the past year, but that it felt great to be able to be back in Oklahoma to play for hometown folks.

Underwood also noted that her time at home was more precious than ever since she had been gone so much after winning *American Idol*. "I don't call my friends or family probably as much as I should," she told the *Tulsa World*, adding, "Usually it's like, 'OK, do I have 20 minutes to spare for a conversation?' And most of the time, I don't. I do still try to call as much as possible."[2]

Underwood's fourth single, "Before He Cheats," provided a major boost for her when she performed it on the ACM Awards show on CBS in May 2006. It was a change in direction for the singer but received good reviews from her performance. Cowritten by Chris Tompkins and Josh Kear, it departed from her previous sweet hometown girl songs with a fervor. The song portrays a woman scorned who is out for revenge. In the video for the tune, Underwood depicted a young woman who decides that instead of creating a scene with her ex-boyfriend, she will just take out her anger on his truck instead. Despite the realistic portrayal of the angry woman who has been done wrong, Underwood assured Westwood One that she was not like that in real life! "I'm not an angry person. I get irritated. And then I think I become a smart aleck."[3]

The video, again directed by Roman White, was shot in various locations around Nashville. It made history on GAC when it debuted at number one. It stayed at the top of the CMT Video Countdown for five weeks and then went on to cross over to premier on MTV's *Total Request Live* in April 2006. Underwood's feat was only the second time a country music video had premiered on this show. Jessica Simpson had the honor of having the first one when she released "These Boots Are Made for Walkin'." It landed the singer a 2007 MTV Video Music Award nomination for the Best New Artist category. The video also gave her multiple wins at the CMT Video Awards on April 16, 2007. She took home Video of the Year and Female Video of the Year, while White received a Director of the Year trophy.

The change in tone didn't deter fans in the least; the song spent five weeks at the top of *Billboard*'s Country Songs chart and went top 10 on the Hot AC chart, making it the first single since Faith Hill's "The Way You Love Me" to do so. It made similar forays into the magazine's Top 40 chart, reaching the top 10 for the first time for a country single since Shania Twain did so in 1999 with "That Don't Impress Me Much." "Before He Cheats" stayed on the *Billboard* Hot 100 chart for 64 weeks, making it the fourth-longest charting single on the Hot 100, following LeAnn Rimes's "How Do I Live," Jewel's "You Were Meant For Me/Foolish Games" and Jason Mraz's "I'm Yours." It remains the second longest running hit of the decade in mid-2010. It was the RIAA's first country single to be certified double Platinum, marking two million downloads in digital sales. It also became a Platinum Mastertone.

When it was determined that "Before He Cheats" might be played on pop stations, a discussion ensued that perhaps they should go back in the studio to make the single more radio-station friendly to that market. Underwood was adamant that she didn't want to have to do that to get the airplay. She told Entertainment Weekly, "I didn't have to put my foot down, thank goodness. I hate it when country artists do that. You're listening to a song on one station and you turn it and you hear a different version? It's like, 'All right, it's not good enough for everybody this way, so let's change it to make it good enough.'"[4]

The singer says that even on songs by one of her favorite performers, Shania Twain, she prefers the country version to the pop ones that the Canadian singer did. And when Underwood performed "Before He Cheats" on Saturday Night Live, she did the original version, not a different one that might be perceived as more palatable for the SNL audience. The singer made her debut appearance on the show on March 24, 2007, guesting with football star Peyton Manning of the Indianapolis Colts. In addition to "Before He Cheats," she also sang "Wasted."

Underwood performed "Before He Cheats" on the 40th annual CMA Awards on November 6, 2006, which aired on ABC. This was also her first year for nominations from the Country Music Association and she had four—Female Vocalist, Horizon Award, Single of the Year, and Music Video of the Year, all for "Jesus, Take the Wheel." Songwriters Hillary Lindsey, Brett James, and Gordon Sampson were also nominated for Song of the Year for that hit single. Underwood took home Female Vocalist of the Year and the Horizon Award, which goes to the artist that has had the most activity in their career in the previous year.

The 2006 CMA Awards were not without controversy. When Underwood won Female Vocalist, cameras were panning the area and happened to capture Faith Hill mouthing "What?" in apparent dismay as she stood by the side of the stage. Hill was also nominated for the award. The next day Hill issued a statement through her publicist stating, "The idea that I would act disrespectful towards a fellow musician is unimaginable to me. For this to become a focus of attention given the talent gathered is utterly ridiculous. Carrie is a talented and deserving female vocalist of the year."

People who knew Hill quickly came to her defense, saying she was just being playful while the nominations were being read and playful after the winner was announced. Hill had been laughing as the nominees were read. Underwood was very gracious about the incident, saying that she didn't think Hill was trying to be mean to her, and the two women quickly put the incident aside. The media and fans kept it going for awhile, though, as all sides weighed in on whether or not Hill was really upset that Underwood won the award.

The Academy of Country Music (ACM) and the Country Music Association (CMA) both are trade organizations that promote country music. ACM is based in Los Angeles and CMA is in Nashville. In 2004 the ACM awards were moved to Las Vegas, where they continue to be held. The CMA Awards have traditionally been held in Nashville, though in 2005 they did originate from New York City for a one-time-only event. Members of either organization have to earn a major portion of their income from country music. It is very prestigious for an artist to be invited to perform on either of these awards shows, especially a newcomer like Underwood. Her popularity from *American Idol* and the chart and sales success she had from her first album and singles were certainly deciding factors in producers of both shows inviting her to be a part of each event.

Underwood continued her winning streak on November 21 when the American Music Awards gave her the Favorite New Artist trophy at its annual awards show, broadcast over ABC from the Shrine Auditorium in Los Angeles. This award was distinctive in that it was an award in the all-genre category. The other artists nominated were Chamillionaire and Pussycat Dolls.

Underwood continued her winning streak when the 49th annual Grammy awards were presented on February 11, 2007. She had several nominations, including the all-genre Song of the Year for "Jesus, Take the Wheel." She was nominated in the all-genre Artist of the Year category, up against James Blunt, Chris Brown, Imogen Heap, and Corinne Bailey Rae. She was also nominated for Best Female Country Vocal Performance. Songwriters Hillary Lindsey, Brett James, and Gordon Sampson were nominated for Song of the Year for "Jesus, Take the Wheel." Her biggest win was Artist of the Year. She told the *Grammy* magazine that she couldn't believe that she had been nominated for multiple Grammy awards the first year she was eligible. "I honestly didn't hold out much hope for the Best New Artist Award because the competition was just too fierce. . . . But when I heard my name called . . . all I can remember is being numb from excitement and adrenaline! Since then there have been many awards and I hope that there will be a few more nominations in the future, but you only get one year to be nominated for this amazing award! If I never win another one . . . I will always have the Best New Artist Grammy Award in my cabinet to gaze upon!"[5] When she won, Underwood was obviously overcome with emotion while thanking her family, God, *American Idol* creator Simon Fuller, the songwriters, and anyone else who had anything to do with the album or the blessed year she had.

Both Underwood and the songwriters took home awards for wins in their respective categories. The singer was also included in the special compilation album *2007 Grammy Nominees*, released by BMG Records, which featured "Jesus, Take the Wheel," along with the Dixie Chicks "Not Ready to Make Nice," Sheryl Crow's "You Can Close Your Eyes," John Legend's "Save Room," and Gnarls Barkley's "Crazy." The CD was declared Gold on February 26, 2007, just a month after its release.

After the success of the first four singles from *Some Hearts*, Underwood's record label took a giant step and released a fifth single from the album, "Wasted," on April 11, 2007. The singer went back to Hillary Lindsey along with songwriting partners Marv Green and Troy Verges for the tune, which was certified an RIAA Gold Digital Single on February 13, 2008. The song continued the success of the previous singles, climbing to the top of *Billboard*'s Country Songs chart. Underwood became the first female singer to release four number-one hits from their debut CD. In 2006, "Before He Cheats" and "Jesus, Take the Wheel" together spent 11 weeks at the number one spot on the Hot Country Songs. That was the longest any female artist has stayed at the top of the *Billboard* chart in a calendar year in the more than 60-year history of the magazine's following country singles airplay.

The singer's debut album, *Some Hearts*, released on November 15, 2005, became the highest-debuting album by a new artist in country music in the history of Nielsen SoundScan, selling 314,549 units. It was declared Gold, with sales of 500,000 units, on December 9, 2005. That same day it received its Platinum certification, for one million units sold. Not quite a month later, on January 6, 2006, it was certified double Platinum, marking the fastest double platinum certification for a country album. RIAA also recognized the album as the best-selling solo female country debut in its history. *Some Hearts* stayed at the top of the *Billboard* charts for 15 of the first 18 weeks of its release. It was the best-selling female country album from 2005 to 2007. During that time period it was at the top of the charts for 27 weeks.

The album didn't stop there. It continued to receive additional million-selling certifications, topping out on January 2, 2007, with sales of 7,000 albums, making it the best-selling solo debut album of any female in country music history. Underwood also became the best-selling album competitor among *American Idol* contestants. After being released on November 15, 2005, *Some Hearts* had stayed at the top of the *Billboard* album charts for a total of 20 weeks. The album continued to sell as Underwood's subsequent albums were released.

While album and single sales, and radio airplay, are a major indication of an artist's popularity, awards are another way to tell just how much saturation a singer has made in their market. Underwood began garnering nominations and awards with her very first endeavors. In addition to the previously mentioned awards, *Some Hearts* received *Billboard*'s Top Country Album in 2006 and 2007, making Underwood the first female artist in the magazine's history to receive back-to-back awards for that category. The only other artist to accomplish the same feat was Charlie Rich, in 1973 and 1974, for his mega recording *Behind Closed Doors*. Underwood also won 2006's Album of the Year and Country Album of the Year. The former was a great honor for Carrie, as many times country artists get overlooked in markets outside of country music. At the 2006 *Billboard* Music Awards, *Some Hearts* took home Album of the Year and Country Album of the Year trophies. "Inside Your Heaven" was named the Top Selling Hot 100 Song and Top Selling Country Single at the 2005 *Billboard* awards.

The Canadian Country Music Association (CCMA) presented the songwriters of "Jesus, Take the Wheel" with its SOCAN Songwriters of the Year, and the Nashville Songwriters Association International (NSAI) awarded the tune its Song of the Year honors. The American

Society of Composers, Authors and Publishers (ASCAP) also named it
Song of the Year.

"Before He Cheats" also chalked up multiple awards for Underwood
and the writers of the song. On April 16, 2007, it received three trophies
at the CMT Music Awards, held at Belmont University's Curb Events
Center in Nashville. She walked away with Female Video of the Year and
CMT Video of the Year for "Before He Cheats." Roman White received
the Director of the Year for that video. Underwood performed "Wasted"
during the 42nd annual Academy of Country Music Awards broadcast
live on CBS from the MGM Grand in Las Vegas. She also took home
awards for Top Female Vocalist; Album of the Year, for *Some Hearts*; and
Video, for "Before He Cheats." The song had also been nominated for
Single and Song of the year. She also presented the New Top Female
Vocalist award to her friend, Miranda Lambert.

ASCAP presented the writers of "Before He Cheats," Josh Kear and
Chris Tompkins, with Song of the Year on October 15, 2007, the second time that one of Underwood's tunes had been so honored. They
shared the award with Dave Berg and his song, "If You're going through
Hell (Before the Devil Even Knows)," recorded by Rodney Atkins. On
November 7, 2007, Underwood received two awards during the 41st annual CMA Awards on ABC—she kept her Female Vocalist title and
took Single of the Year honors for "Before He Cheats." She had also
been nominated for Video of the Year, and the writers, Chris Tompkins
and Josh Kear, were nominated for Song of the Year. The next week, on
November 16, Underwood was invited to be a part of the Oklahoma
Centennial Spectacular at the Ford Center in Oklahoma City. She was
proud to be a part of the tribute to her home state, alongside such celebrities as Garth Brooks, Reba McEntire, Toby Keith, Blake Shelton,
Vince Gill, Amy Grant, Jimmy Webb, Byron Berline, and Patti Page.
Two nights later, November 18, Underwood was still picking up awards.
This time she was attending the American Music Awards, where she re-
ceived awards for both of her nominations—Female Vocalist and Album
for *Some Hearts*.

Underwood was the owner of many trophies by now, so those journalists who are naturally curious asked if she kept them in her house
in Nashville. She told the *Tulsa World* that while she could not give
an exact count of how many awards she had won, she definitely had a

Carrie Underwood accepts the
Favorite Country Female Art-
ist award at the American Music
Awards in Los Angeles on Nov. 18,
2007. (AP Photo/Mark J.
Terrill.)

special place for them. "I display them all proudly. They're not all over my house, because I feel like my house is where I go to get away from myself. But I do have a cabinet where I keep everything all shiny and pretty and it's all centralized to one location. So, if I ever want to go look at them, I can."[6]

Underwood closed out the year with Dick Clark. She performed two songs, "All-American Girl" and "Before He Cheats," on "Dick Clark's New Year's Rockin' Eve" on ABC. Joining Underwood on the special were friends Taylor Swift, Miley Cyrus, and Ryan Seacrest.

NOTES

1. Pam Green, Carrie Underwood Interview, Westwood One Radio Network, November 12, 2008.

2. John Wooley, "Idol Eyes a Show at Home," *Tulsa World*, June 4, 2006.

3. Pam Green, Carrie Underwood Interview.

4. Dave Karger, "Carrie Underwood: A Very Private Idol Speaks Out," *Entertainment Weekly*, October 26, 2007.

5. "Best New Artist 2007: Carrie Underwood," *Grammy Magazine*, http://www.grammy.com, January 11, 2010.

6. Jennifer Chancellor, "Very Excited: Carrie Underwood at the BOK," *Tulsa World*, October 26, 2008.

Chapter 6

LOOK AT ME

While Underwood was busy taking home awards to put on the newly built shelves in her Nashville home, she was also discovering just what it meant to be a celebrity. The cute girl-next-door who had tried out for *American Idol* had become a high-profile entertainer, and all of a sudden, every move she made was talked about by the media and her fans. No amount of advice can prepare an individual for what it's like to be under such constant scrutiny.

If one takes a look at Underwood's image when she first appeared on *American Idol*, and the image she has today, it is easy to see that it has changed dramatically. On *Idol* she first came out in basic bought-off-the-rack clothes that she brought with her to the auditions. They were nice and what one would expect from a college student who had done some performing but had not been exposed to the fashions of the celebrity world. As the show progressed, and fashion experts worked with her, the image changed from week to week. She went from cowboy shirt and jeans with straight hair to curly hair and a sexy black strapless dress. The image consultants on the show didn't miss out on trying her in big hair with black jacket, jeans, and belt one night, and a sequined dress for another look. Another evening saw her in jeans with cropped jacket, sequined scarf, and soft waves. The final night they had her in a leopard print semi-see-through dress and curly hair.

Once she signed with a major label, Underwood's look changed even more. Most of the time one of the first things a manager or publicist at the label does is take the new artist to an image consultant, who gives them a new look for their new career. This person basically decides what it will take to "sell" the new artist to the general public who will be buying their records. If torn jeans and tee shirts are in style, that's what they will dress the artist in. If it's more appropriate to have them in cowboy hat and western shirt and boots, that's the style they will adopt. The image consultants took Underwood in a brand new direction. She was soon sporting even more fashionable attire and cool new hairstyles, perhaps none more surprising than the shorts she started wearing in concert or the plunging necklines that began appearing on formal clothes she wore to award shows. It was a sleeker, new Underwood that greeted the American public, and they loved it. Suddenly Underwood was wearing dresses by major fashion designers, including the Kwiat Diamond Dress designed by David Rodriguez that she wore to the 2006 CMA Awards show. Everything she did during this time, from the new clothes to makeup and hairstyle, helped shape the image that was presented by the record label and her management team to her fans. Because Underwood tends to be hands-on, she no doubt had a say in this image, but it was a definite change for the college student from Checotah who walked on that stage in St. Louis, Missouri, to audition for *American Idol*.

That doesn't take away from the girl-next-door image that she was described as having on *Idol*. Underwood had a solid background from her family in Checotah, Oklahoma. When she was described as the "girl-next-door," she really did fit the good, clean, all-American image that phrase implies. She and her two sisters had a great family who supported each other in their endeavors, and the small-town upbringing gave her a sense of community, loyalty, honesty, and ethics. When she became a contestant on *American Idol*, she had never flown before her initial trip to California. She has maintained that image throughout her career, never getting involved in any scandals and always having a positive image to present to her fans, whether they be young children or their parents and grandparents. Underwood is very aware that a lot of young girls look up to her and she tries hard to present a positive image for them.

During *American Idol,* the singer had stated that she hoped to live in Checotah. She soon realized that she was going to be required to be in Nashville so much of the time, she had to make a major decision when it came to buying her first home. Living in Nashville made more sense because her band was there, and the city is a center hub for heading out in any direction for her tour. It wasn't long after her *Idol* win that Underwood bought a home in a normal neighborhood outside of Nashville, shortly before the release of her first album, *Some Hearts.* She said she was tired of living in hotels and ready to establish a residency in the place where she will spend much of her time. She chose a modest three-bedroom home, one she says "wouldn't break the bank" if her career didn't maintain its momentum. Underwood and a friend live in the home along with her dog, Ace. "It's not a gated community, which might've been a little mistake on my part, but since I live by myself, I wanted to have neighbors," Underwood told the *Tulsa World* right after purchasing the new home, before she added a roommate. "I didn't want to get stuck out in the middle of nowhere, where a crazy person could break into my house and steal me."[1]

Nashville is a good jump from Checotah for Underwood. It's one of those towns that has grown in the past decade but has managed to maintain its southern charm and friendly atmosphere. Dubbed "the Athens of the South" for its numerous learning institutions, including Vanderbilt University and Belmont University, the city has maintained its small-town feel while its population increased to more than 600,000 by 2008. The city, also the capitol of Tennessee, was founded in 1779 by James Robertson, John Donelson, and a group of Wataugan Indians. The party came down the Cumberland River and established Fort Nashborough on its banks. The city was named after American Revolutionary War hero Francis Nash, but there are many nods to Robertson and Donelson in the city's suburbs and roads. Because of its location as a river port, the town grew quickly. Later, when railroads came through, it became a center for that means of transportation as well. It was incorporated in 1806, when it became the county seat of Davidson County. Again because of its accessibility, Nashville was a very desired location during the Civil War and fell into the hands of Union troops in 1862. After the war it rebounded quickly, getting back into shipping and trading but increasing its base as a manufacturing hub as well. It is also a huge printing center and is home to several major insurance companies.

In 1925 a small radio show, dubbed the *Grand Ole Opry*, became the impetus that sparked a new industry for Nashville—country music. It was originally owned by the National Life & Accident Insurance Company, but sold to Gaylord Enterprises in the 1990s. Later dubbed Music City U.S.A., Nashville now boasts a thriving music scene for country, blue-grass, Americana, Christian, blues, and alternative singers and bands. To-day the *Grand Ole Opry* is the longest-running radio show in the world.

Nashville's music industry has also grown. Acuff-Rose, founded by Roy Acuff and Fred Rose, was one of the first music (song) publishing com-panies in the city when it opened in October 1942. Prior to that, how-ever, Nashville was already making its niche as a music town. In 1824 a hymnal was produced there, making the way for gospel and Christian music to find its own niche in the city. In the 1850s a tune by Charles Benson, "Here's Your Mule," was written and became very popular during the Civil War. It was published in Nashville. By the early 20th century, Nashville could boast its own music publishing company, a chapter of the American Federation of Musicians, and a certified songwriter. The Fisk Jubilee Singers also brought recognition to Nashville as a music town as they traveled across the United States performing and raising money for Fisk University.

In 1892 a building was constructed in Nashville that would remain a major force in its music history to this day. The Union Gospel Taber-nacle was built to give riverboat captain turned preacher and evangelist Tom Ryman his base for saving thousands of souls. When he died it was decided to name the building after him, so it became the Ryman Audito-rium. It soon became known as the Carnegie Hall of the South because of its great acoustics, and many popular entertainers of the day have per-formed there, including Judy Garland, Betty Grable, Victor Borge, and Enrico Caruso. In 1943 it became home to the Grand Ole Opry, which remained there until 1974 when a new Grand Ole Opry house was built at the Opryland U.S.A. complex. After years of disrepair, it was refur-bished and is once again a popular music venue, with performances by everyone including Kid Rock, Neil Diamond, B.B. King, Hootie and the Blowfish, the Trans-Siberian Orchestra, and the Black Crowes. The Opry returns to the Ryman every year for its winter performance schedule.

After Elvis Presley signed with RCA, that company established a branch office in Nashville, one that is now known as Sony Nashville, home to superstars like Brad Paisley, Alan Jackson, Gretchen Wilson, Jake Owen, Chuck Wicks, and Carrie Underwood. Soon recording studios began to find brisk business following the opening of Owen Bradley's Sixteenth Avenue Sound in the early 1950s. Music was becoming such a prominent business that David Cobb, a deejay on WSM Radio, referred to Nashville on one of his broadcasts as "Music City U.S.A." and the city continues to have that moniker today. Chet Atkins was appointed to run RCA's newly built studio in 1957. Together he and Bradley began producing a style of country music that was to become known as the Nashville sound.

Acuff-Rose had its own record company for a while, Hickory Records, and major corporations including MCA, Capitol, and Warner Brothers opened offices there. The gospel music business is also thriving in Nashville, where numerous record labels release albums on superstars like Steven Curtis Chapman, Amy Grant, Michael W. Smith, Natalie Grant, Nicole Mullen, MercyMe, and Third Day. Other genres of music flourish in Music City U.S.A., including bluegrass, alternative, the blues, and Americana. Not only is Nashville home to the Country Music Association and the Gospel Music Association, the International Bluegrass Music Association moved its offices there in 2003. The Americana Music Association was formed and held its first awards show in 2002. There are singer/songwriter, indie rock, and independent artist movements as well, which can be heard in venues like Grimey's, 12th & Porter, Douglas Corner, 3rd & Lindsley, the Bluebird Café, and the Basement. Visitors to these clubs might be surprised at who shows up as special guest performers, because Nashville is also full and/or part-time home to a number of stars, including Sheryl Crow, Kid Rock, Donna Summers, and Steve Cropper.

That group of artists, and country music's top-selling stars of today, are very different from the first singers and songwriters who made their way to Music City. Many of them, including Hank Williams, Ernest Tubb, Patsy Cline, Loretta Lynn, Willie Nelson, and Waylon Jennings, worked their way to Nashville by playing numerous honky-tonks and dives along the way. Many a story has been told about playing behind a fence of chicken wire to keep the broken bottles from flying onstage while the band was playing. At the very least, once a country entertainer arrived in Nashville, they had played all the clubs, churches, and county fairs in their neck of the woods. They could walk onstage and entertain a crowd, whether they were at the Grand Ole Opry or the local high school auditorium. Today, so some in Nashville complain, the newcomers are not entertainers, just singers who put down their music to release on records; singers who must learn to be entertainers while they earn thousands of dollars a night more than the men and women who went before them.

Underwood heard her share of this type of talk as well. She or others on her team heard that she didn't have the experience behind her; she hadn't paid her dues; she wasn't ready to headline a tour. "It kind of hurts my feelings because nobody in the business went through what the contestants on 'American Idol' went through. That's a whole 'nother kind of dues-payin' right there," Underwood told *CMT Insider*.[2]

She went on to reiterate how lucky she is to be doing what she dreamed of doing. "You know, I'll be the first person to say I don't deserve [to be] where I am. I am so, so lucky to be where I am, and I'm so thankful every single day that all this wonderful stuff has happened to me, but I definitely went through a different kind of 'dues-paying' portion of my life—and that was called 'American Idol'."[3]

Actually Underwood fits right in with the other stars who live in Music City U.S.A. Most of the major entertainers, from Elvis Presley to James Brown, the Everly Brothers, Sir Paul McCartney, James Taylor, Jimi Hendrix, Jimmy Buffet, Bob Dylan, Nelly, and Jon Bon Jovi, have gone there to write with the town's songwriters, record in its studios, and perform in one of its many venues.

The town continues to grow in the area of arts and sports. The new Frist Art Museum brought a much needed place for art lovers to the town, and a new downtown public library continued the growth of the area along the riverbanks. The Nashville Symphony has a new home at the Schermerhorn Symphony Center, and the Country Music Hall of Fame and Museum opened in its new downtown location in 2001. Five years later the Musicians Hall of Fame and Museum opened its doors near downtown. Unfortunately the Musicians Hall of Fame is gone due to construction of the new convention center which is being built downtown, and its new location and fate have not been decided since much of its memorabilia was lost in Nashville's spring flood in 2010.

The Tennessee Titans football team moved to its new home, LP Field, in 1999. Nashville also boasts the Nashville Predators hockey team and the Nashville Sounds Minor League Baseball Class AAA team. A new convention center, which will be larger and have the capability to book bigger conventions and meetings, is currently being built downtown across from the Country Music Hall of Fame.

While Nashville is a much larger city than Checotah, Underwood says it feels like a small town to her. "I love living in Nashville. I don't have, like, paparazzi following me you know, and they don't in Nashville. When I go places, it's a little bit different but I mean here people are great. I live in a good neighborhood and nobody really messes with me at all," she told Westwood One Radio. "I'm lucky to live here."[4]

The singer has managed to maintain that hometown girl image and has become a great example for young people in America. She is a vegetarian, she puts a great amount of effort into charity work including rescuing animals, and she has never been arrested for drugs or alcohol abuse or anything else that would put her reputation on the line. She has thousands of young fans who adore her and as many thousand parents who are thankful that their child has found a celebrity who also stands for good old-fashioned American values—God, country, and family.

On her 2009 album *Play On*, Underwood recorded a song titled "Change." It basically says what she believes, that no matter how big or small, people can always make a difference when they reach out to someone in need. She has said that she hopes she will be able to encourage people to help others through the lyrics of this tune.

Underwood made some decisions early in life that are good examples of why young people admire her. At the age of 13 Underwood decided to become a vegetarian. PETA (People for the Ethical Treatment of Animals) voted her the "World's Sexiest Vegetarian" in 2005 and 2007. Underwood told PETA after her 2007 honor, "Ever since I was little I loved animals. If you told me I could never sing again, I'd say that was horrible but it's not my life. If you told me I could never be around animals again, I would just die."

Underwood says it was an individual choice to become a vegetarian and one that she does not try to push on other people. "I chose that because I grew up on a farm and it just weirds me out (to think about eating meat). I don't preach to other people; I don't tell people they shouldn't eat meat. I take good care of myself and get all the nutrition I need, and if someone has questions I'll answer their questions but I don't push it on anybody. I love the lifestyle, I think I feel better and I never see myself eating meat again."[5]

The singer says she can maintain her vegetarian diet while she's on the road, but it's a little harder to do so in the south. "Oh my gosh, everything's fried and everything's meat, meat, meat. I carry food with me. It's not hard if you know how to do it. Some people would think it's hard but if they hang out with me for awhile they would see what I eat and realize that it's not hard."[6]

While she has never hired a nutritionist to guide her, Underwood says she gets a lot of her information from her own research. "I read a lot, I look things up on the Internet, like how much protein I need to have, how many calories. With the Internet and books that are available, it's very easy to keep up with all that and know how to take care of yourself."[7]

The singer was inadvertently involved in a bit of controversy with PETA in December 2009. She was featured, along with Michelle Obama, Tyra Banks, and Oprah Winfrey, in PETA no-fur ads, which were unveiled at train stops in Washington, D.C. Because Obama had never consented to be in the ads, they did not remain available for very long before they were taken down.

Underwood has four pets—two cats and two dogs, Hastings and Maxwell, Molly and Ace. Ace lives with her in Nashville and travels with her on the bus to her concert dates. The others live with her parents back in Checotah.

The singer doesn't just say she loves animals; she backs that statement by supporting them through various organizations. She has recorded several public service announcements (PSA) for the Humane Society of the United States (HSUS). The organization was established in 1954 and seeks to protect animals against cruelty, exploitation, and neglect while continuing to explore the human–animal bond. This is the organization that is often seen on television when a raid is done on a local puppy mill, or when a large number of animals are rescued from the confines of cruelty such as starvation or terrible living conditions.

In her hometown of Checotah, Underwood formed a foundation called C.A.T.S., the acronym for Checotah Animal, Town, and School

Foundation, which provides charitable funds for her hometown area. In the January 2010 issue of *Self*, Underwood said that she plans to give away all her money before she leaves this earth. In regards to C.A.T.S., she said, "I'm looking forward to doing a lot of good for a community that's a big part of why I am who I am." Underwood says she's had so many good things happen to her that she feels that it is definitely time to start giving back.[8]

"I was born to family that always had animals," Underwood explains about her love for the animal kingdom to Westwood One. "When I was growing up I had cats, dogs, rabbits, a pet duck, an iguana, fish, hamsters . . . I had it all. My first pet was a dog that was already at home when I was born. Her name was Fifi. She was a mix but she was a protector. Now I have a rat terrier who is nine pounds of ferociousness, and I also have cats and dogs."[9]

Underwood says she was born with an instinct to love and protect animals. "Ever since I was little I always loved animals. They are completely helpless and they need us to take care of them. I think some of the worst people in the world are people who don't take care of animals. I worked at a veterinarian clinic; it was my last 'job' that I had before I was back at school. Some of the people who would bring their animals, it was horrendous and made me sick to my stomach and so sad. I'm a big big advocator of getting animals from shelters and spaying and neutering your pets please. My two cats and my dog Molly were pets I found."[10]

In February 2010, Underwood agreed to do a public service announcement for Pedigree dog food, the sponsor for her "Play On" tour, to talk about the company's adoption drive. Underwood told Pedigree, "I can't imagine life without my dog, Ace. Dogs are just beautiful souls that don't want a thing from you. Ace is special because he loves me for no reason other than I love him back." Pedigree's program was aimed at educating people about the plight of homeless dogs in America and makes donations of food and funding to further that effort.

On August 28, 2009, Underwood took $117,000 worth of musical instruments to her hometown's high school. Her visit was a surprise to the students gathered during an assembly at the school. "I'm so proud to have come from such a wonderful community that helped shape me as a person," Underwood said during the presentation. "I can think of nothing better than to share the gift of music with the students in my hometown. It's great to be able to give back in a way that can truly better the lives of these kids and help create dreams and opportunities."[11]

Underwood also praised her first music teacher, Kathy Cooper, who she said had been a positive influence in her life. She invited a student, 11-year-old Kenedee Rittenhouse, to join her onstage after the girl did an impromptu performance of Underwood's hit "So Small" before the assembly got underway and before she knew the singer was backstage. "Singing with her was a one in a million opportunity and it was so awesome," Rittenhouse told the *Tulsa World*. "She hugged me after and said 'Great job.'"[12]

Underwood urged the students to do what they loved. She later told the newspaper, "I think it's great for kids to see that they can do anything. I want to help teach them to be responsible for their futures, to be great and to follow their dreams." The instruments were a joint gift from the singer's C.A.T.S. Foundation and the Academy of Country Music's Lifting Lives program.[13]

Underwood also took part in a statewide effort to promote reading. She joined Toby Keith, author Dana Dunbar, and others on posters for the Oklahoma Library Association's "Read Y'all" literacy campaign. The posters will be distributed throughout schools across the state to encourage people to learn to read.

Another way the singer has given back is through *American Idol*. In 2007 she went to South Africa to visit and perform for schools, orphanages, hospices, and health care centers in and around Johannesburg. The trip was captured on film, and a portion of it was shown on "Idol Gives Back," a special that the popular television show does each year. She also recorded a version of the Pretenders classic "I'll Stand By You" to sell on iTunes, with proceeds going to the "Idol Gives Back" charity effort. She is quoted in a bio on GAC-TV's (Great American Television) Web site saying, "Everybody has the power to do something, to be a contributing force, and I would rather people look back on my life and say, 'She made the world a better place.' We can all do things like that, and I believe that when opportunities arise for you to do good, you should do good."[14]

In the spring of 2009, Underwood undertook another humanitarian trip to Africa. On May 12, images from that trip were shown on *American*

Idol, featuring her hit single "So Small." In December 2009, Underwood, along with 19 Records and Sony Music Nashville, presented "Idol Gives Back" with a check for $200,000, proceeds from the sales of the singer's recording of "Home Sweet Home." That song was the tune the contestants sang as their final performance on season eight of *American Idol.*

Underwood also did a "Protect Your Pets" PSA for the national organization Do Something, which encourages youth to believe they have the power to make a difference in the world. The group's aim is to inspire, support, and celebrate a generation of doers. They address causes that are important to teens, such as healthy eating, recycling, and caring for pets. The organization is a support system for teens who have ideas that they think will better the world around them, and it offers not only financial support when possible but encouragement to these young men and women to follow their dreams of helping create a better world around them.

Underwood lends her voice to benefit cancer research. She was a part of the song, "Just Stand Up," which was released in 2008 to benefit Stand Up to Cancer. On September 5 of that year, Underwood joined LeAnn Rimes, Miley Cyrus, Sheryl Crow, Mariah Carey, Melissa Etheridge, and Sugarland on the television special "Stand Up to Cancer," which was a fundraising effort that ran on the three major networks: ABC, CBS, and NBC.

She also is a supporter of the United Services Organization (USO), which is a private, nonprofit organization whose mission is to provide morale, welfare, and recreation-type services to men and women in uniform. Underwood joined celebrities including Bob Hope, Gary Sinese, Kid Rock, and Stevie Nicks in supporting U.S. soldiers. She performed with the USO Christmas Tour in Iraq in 2006, leaving on December 11 and returning on December 18. Her first performance was at Camp Adder, Talil Air Base, on December 14. She also performed for 2,000 American troops at Camp Arifjan in Kuwait. Not only did Underwood perform, she took time to talk with the men and women who came to the shows and signed autographs for them for several hours after each performance. She said she was excited about going on her first USO trip and welcomed the opportunity to bring entertainment to the men and women in the military. On August 14, 2009, Underwood took time to perform another concert for the troops, this one a little closer to home.

Along with Hank Williams Jr., John Rich, and Jake Owen, the singer performed a free "Salute to the Troops" show for soldiers at Ford Campbell, Kentucky, just about an hour's drive from Nashville.

Like many country celebrities, Underwood supports St. Jude Children's Research Hospital in Memphis, Tennessee. On January 15, 2010, she joined Steve Azar, Danny Gokey, Jewel, Little Big Town, Lynyrd Skynyrd, Joe Nichols, Randy Owen, and Darryl Worley to visit the hospital and spend time with the kids who were undergoing treatment there. It was the kick-off weekend for the annual Country Cares for St. Jude Kids fund-raising radiothon. Country stations across the United States take part in the event, which has raised more than $365 million for the hospital.

"I can't say that I understand anything anybody is going through here," Underwood says in a video posted on YouTube, continuing with a catch in her voice. "You put yourself in that position and what if it was my kids. It's a tough thing to think about."[15] She went on to say that she's all about being involved in places like St. Jude, which give people hope and do good in the world. In an interview with USA Today, she explained that St. Jude is not like other hospitals. "When you walk in the door of St. Jude it is happy. There are pictures on the wall—kid-created pictures—and it is not like a hospital. It is not a cold environment."[16]

St. Jude is a pediatric treatment and research facility whose discoveries have changed how the world treats children with cancer and other catastrophic diseases. It is a place where cutting-edge research and revolutionary discoveries happen often. The survival rate for acute lymphoblastic leukemia, the most common of the childhood cancers, increased from 4 percent in 1962 to 94 percent after St. Jude was established.

St. Jude is America's second-largest health-care charity. The hospital was founded by entertainer Danny Thomas and named after Saint Jude Thaddeus, the Catholic patron saint of hospitals. Thomas's premise for the hospital is that no child should die in the dawn of life. The hospital has treated children from not only the United States but more than 70 countries as well. Patients are accepted for admission and are treated without regard to the family's ability to pay.

In November 2006 Underwood donated the one-of-a kind Kwiat Diamond Dress that she wore to the Country Music Association Awards to charity, with a portion going to the Humane Society of the United

States (HSUS) for their Rural Area Veterinary Associates Program. The dress was a collaborative effort by Kwiat Diamonds and fashion designer David Rodriguez and was worn by Underwood on the red carpet, as well as when she accepted awards for Female Vocalist of the Year and the Horizon Award for best new artist. The dress, which had nearly 800 Kwiat diamonds of over 108 carats just on the straps of the dress, was valued at $850,000. The fashion piece was made of platinum gray Chantilly lace lined in silk charmeuse. Another portion of the sale went to Kwiat's charity of choice, the Make-A-Wish Foundation.

Underwood has become somewhat of a fashion maven since her ascent to celebrity status. While she says she is willing to wear anything onstage, even makeup, she prefers sweats from Victoria's Secret when she's lounging around on the bus or at home. She says she gets some of her confidence in trying different styles together from one of favorite artists, Dolly Parton. "I would never attempt to pull off Dolly's wardrobe, but her confidence is enviable," Underwood said. "She always makes it work." The singer goes on to say that she would wear boots no matter what kind of music she sings, adding she likes to mix them with cute dresses so she can be both country and stylish. When it comes to awards shows and major appearances, Underwood is always stylish. Among the top designers she's gone to for her red carpet and awards show dresses are Zuhair Murad, Pamella Roland, Christian Cota, Daniel Swarovski, Jenny Packham, Milly, Mary Norton, Cinta by John Hardy, and Badgley Mischka.

One advantage of being a celebrity with style is receiving an invitation to Fashion Week in New York City in the fall. On September 6, 2007, Underwood and Martina McBride were invited to be part of the Fashion Rocks concert at Radio City Music Hall in New York. The event was filmed for a CBS television special that aired the next night. Also on the show were Alicia Keys, Aerosmith, Santana, and Usher.

In March 2009 Underwood joined Brooke Shields, Eva Longoria, Laurent Hutton, and Angelica Huston in an ad campaign for Badgley Mischka's 20th anniversary. The ads, shot by premier photographer Annie Leibovitz, were in the April issue of magazines including *Vogue, Instyle,* and *Harper's Bazaar.* Commenting on the designer, Underwood said, "I love Badgley Mischka for not only making the most beautiful gowns, but also for bringing together such strong, amazing women to celebrate

20 years of glamour and fashion. I am thrilled to be part of their special anniversary."[17]

While Underwood is all about fashion and looks when she's out in public, she's more a sweats and tee shirt kind of girl at home. She told *Allure* magazine, "I think of 'Carrie Underwood' as being a different person," says the singer. "I'm, like, Carrie in my sweatpants. But 'Carrie Underwood' is a person who can, you know, wear all the fishnets and the corsets. A lot of fun, to be able to be a bad girl, you know?"[18]

In 2008 Underwood appeared in *Shape* magazine's February issue, talking about losing weight. Some bloggers and other media had accused the singer of being chubby, and she told the magazine she was tired of people calling attention to her weight. This was one of the times that Underwood's celebrity caused her to fall under scrutiny when a gain of a few pounds as a young woman in Checotah would never have created a discussion. She talked about her weight loss with *Shape* and what worked for her in dropping the pounds.

"Cardio really helps the pounds melt off and it gives me so much more energy," she said. "Now when I'm performing and running around the stage, it's no big deal, but before I was always gasping for breath. Working out has really paid off onstage. I'm a performer, and yes, being in good shape is part of the package."[19] Underwood cautioned that she would not obsess about her weight. "I don't ever want to get neurotic about my weight. I feel healthy and I know I'm a good size for me. And that's what's important."[20]

Another part of Underwood's life that is wide open to scrutiny is who she dates. From the Dallas Cowboys Quarterback Tony Romo to hockey star Mike Fisher, the singer's fans and critics alike followed her as she sought to find a relationship while living under a microscope. The first high-profile man Underwood became associated with was Romo. The two apparently became acquainted in the latter part of 2006, although Underwood says that they never were officially a couple. They did hang out together for awhile into 2007. The first rumors of a possible romance came after the Dallas Cowboys vs. Philadelphia Eagles game on Christmas Day at Texas Stadium, 2006, where Underwood gave Romo a hug on the field before she went into the stands to watch the game. The Cowboys lost that game, and rumors flew that if Romo had his mind on the game instead of the singer, his team would have won.

Carrie Underwood and Dallas Cowboys quarterback Tony Romo arrive at the 42nd Annual Academy of Country Music Awards on May 15, 2007, in Las Vegas. (AP Photo/Jae C. Hong.)

Romo confirmed the two were dating in an interview with the *Journal Gazette/Times-Courier* in Charleston, Illinois, where he played football prior to hitting the pros.

The two seemed like a couple, despite Underwood being adamant that they were just friends. Romo flew to Nashville to celebrate the singer's 24th birthday in March 2007, and she flew to Dallas for his 27th birthday in April. In May he was her date to the Academy of Country Music Awards show in Las Vegas, Nevada. Later in 2007 rumors started that the two were ending their relationship, whatever it was. People.com reported that Romo had asked for a hiatus during football season, September through January, so he could concentrate on his game.

Both Romo and Underwood were gracious about their breakup, with the singer continuing to maintain that indeed the friendship seemed headed toward a relationship, but "He is about football. I don't know if it's that I'm not quite his type or whatever, but I don't think he's at that point in his life where he would be willing to sacrifice football. He hated so much that people thought that he was paying attention to me and that was causing him not to do well." Underwood added, "The Cowboys are still my favorite team, no matter what happens with us."[21] As for Romo, he said of the former *Idol* winner, "I've been lucky to get to know her. We're friends."[22] When Underwood released her single, "Cowboy Casanova," in September 2009, there was much speculation that it was about Romo. She wrote the tune with Mike Elizondo and Brett James, and it is on her third CD release, *Play On.* In the song, she warns a woman to be careful of the man she is dating because he's a cowboy Casanova with blue eyes who only comes out at night. *Esquire* magazine asked Underwood if the song was about Romo and she told them, "No. I would never immortalize a guy that did me wrong. I would never give him that much credit."[23]

After Romo, Underwood went out with actor Chace Crawford of *Gossip Girls* fame. In October 2007, the magazine *OK!* reported that she and Crawford had been seen in a New York City nightclub, the Marquee, and at other popular spots throughout that weekend. In the same timeframe, she was quoted in *People* magazine from an interview in *Seventeen* magazine that she and Romo "are very good friends and I talk to him pretty much every day, whether it's text or whatever. But we were never, like dating."[24]

Underwood was two years older than Crawford, but that didn't seem to bother either of them. Friends suggested they were a good match, since he is from Texas and she from the neighboring state of Oklahoma. Underwood told *People*, "He's really cute. He's got cool hair, he's a nice height and he just has beautiful blue eyes." [25]

Unfortunately, the next spring the two were calling it quits. They ended the relationship in a very technically savvy way—via text message. Underwood said it was mutual and told the magazine *Extra*, "It was like Peace, out." She says the two just realized it wasn't going to work and there were no hard feelings over the breakup.[26]

Underwood told *Extra* that it was hard to maintain a relationship when the people involved are celebrities. "It's difficult while you're dating because people always make a lot bigger deal of things than they actually are."[27] Nevertheless, the singer began dating Ottawa Senators hockey star Mike Fisher after the two met through a friend of a friend in March 21, 2008, when he went backstage at her concert at Scotiabank Place in Ottawa. Fisher acknowledges that the relationship has been good and that he and Underwood find a way to make it work. He says his favorite song from his girlfriend is "Temporary Home," from her 2009 CD *Play On*. He is an obvious admirer of her talent, telling *People* magazine, "She can sing anything—I like it when she sings a good rock song."[28] Fisher also told *People* magazine that Underwood is very committed (to her career) and works extremely hard. "She doesn't get too many days off—a lot less days off than I get. She's always going."[29] Fisher told the *Toronto Sun* that Underwood is only his second "serious" girlfriend, and the singer admitted to Ellen DeGeneres on her show that the hockey player is the longest relationship she's ever had. In fact, she included Fisher in the liner notes to her *Play On* CD, writing, "Thank you (No.) 12 (his jersey number). You are the most amazing addition to my life! You are such a wonderful person and have had such an amazing hand in the building of this album and in the growth of me as a person. I love you so much! You make my life better in every way!" However, Underwood went on to tell DeGeneres, "Call me old fashioned, but the next guy I move in with will be my hubby. Whoever that is. I'm not saying it's going to be him (Fisher)."[30]

Underwood was quoted in the *Tulsa World* about what her parents thought of Fisher. "They love me and I would hope my parents would think 'We raised a good, smart girl, so she's going to do the right thing no matter what it is.'"[31] In December 2009, Underwood and Fisher announced that they were engaged. The couple confirmed their engagement after a relative of Underwood's congratulated her via Twitter. Fisher confirmed the news to a Canadian sports reporter who asked him about it before the Senators' game with the Boston Bruins. "We're both obviously excited and very happy," he said. The sports celebrity proposed to Underwood on December 20, at his home surrounded by family and friends, according to CMT.[32]

On January 25, Fisher made an appearance with Underwood at the Bell Sens Soiree children's benefit in Ottawa, Ontario, Canada. The couple walked the red carpet together for the first time since they announced their engagement in December. By June rumors were surfacing that the wedding would be held in Tennessee in July, but neither Carrie nor Mike would confirm a date. Underwood told Tony Greco on his radio show, *Grecosize*, that the two were finding it hard to get together to plan the big event. "It seems like this past year when I have time off they have away games. . . . We're hoping the summer will be some nice time for us to spend consecutive days together." Underwood added, "Our schedules don't provide us too much time to get married and have time to really

Carrie Underwood and Mike Fisher
arrive at the Grammy Awards on
January 31, 2010, in Los Angeles.
(AP Photo/Chris Pizzello.)

enjoy being married. We're trying to really work it out and move some stuff around."[33]

Underwood also said that initially Fisher told her he didn't care about the plans for the wedding, that she could just do them and tell him about it. Now she says despite him telling her to do whatever she wants, she'll ask him something and he'll say "No" and then he'll give her an opinion. "I think he's going to be more involved than he initially thought he wanted to be, which is good. I need help."

The engagement ring, with a round diamond said to be between three and five carets, has been valued from $150,000 up to a million. According to Mo Charania, a gemologist and owner of Jubilee Jewelers at Bayshore Shopping Centre in Ottawa, the stone is a center cut round diamond with one row of diamonds around it called micro pave. Charania made the determination after seeing photos of the ring shortly after the engagement. The intricate micro pave settings use very small diamonds that achieve a uniform glitter on the surface of the ring. Sometimes, the tiny claws on the outside can hold 30 or more stones. It was designed by

Johnathon Arndt of Johnathon Arndt Gallery of Jewels, with six locations worldwide. Arndt says he is proud and honored that he was the designer for the flawless yellow diamond engagement ring, adding, "This ring is a symbol of love from Mike Fisher to Carrie Underwood." The singer is no stranger to the beautiful work that Arndt can produce—she has worn Arndt's one-of-a-kind creations at numerous events, including the Academy of Country Music awards and the Country Music Association awards show.

Although the ring has been a topic of conversation ever since Underwood began wearing it, she set the record straight in an interview she did for *Allure* magazine in April 2010. "He could have put a twisty-tie on my finger and that would have worked. He is the person that I see making me happy for the rest of our lives, and he is the person I would do anything for to make him happy. I very well may be the luckiest girl in the world."[34]

Underwood and Fisher were married on July 10, 2010 at the Ritz-Carlton Reynolds Plantation Resort in Greensboro, Georgia. She wore a Chantilly lace and silk organza wedding gown designed by Monique Lhuillier. Not to be outdone, her dog Ace, who travels with her on tour, wore a pink tuxedo decorated with Swarovski crystals. "Mike was like, 'He's in pink. What are you doing," Underwood told *People* magazine, "but he looked so handsome."[35]

After the ceremony, Underwood changed into a strapless Lhuillier cocktail dress. The reason? "The wedding dress was huge and I wanted to get my boogie on, so I had to change," she informed *People*.[36]

Among the invited guests, in addition to the couple's families and members of the Ottawa Senator's hockey team, were Garth Brooks, Faith Hill, and *American Idol* judges Paula Abdul, Randy Jackson, and Simon Cowell.[37]

Fisher told *People* magazine, "[She] looked stunning. I was thanking God for her, for that moment. It's something I'll never forget."[38]

The couple honeymooned on the French Polynesian island of Tahiti, where they snorkeled, swam, and toured the area in a helicopter.[39]

While everyone is thrilled for the couple, Underwood has encountered a few people who are adamant that she not take her husband-to-be away from his native Canada. She admits to *The Edmonton Sun* that the hardest thing for her to get used to in Canada is the snow, because she doesn't get very much of it in her native Checotah or in Nashville, where she currently lives. She hastens to add, however, that for the most part, people have been accepting of the marriage and encouraging as she gets to know his native Canada. "The people I've met here are great, helping me to adjust to life in Canada. And they love Mike. That warms my heart."[40]

Underwood continued, "A woman came up to me at the grocery store and chewed me out, telling me if I thought I was going to take Mike away from Ottawa, I had another think coming, and she wasn't kidding. She let me know she loved him and he was going to stay here, period, no matter what I said. She might have been kidding, but she wasn't being funny."[41] Underwood assures Fisher's fans that the couple will split their time between Nashville in the summer when she's on tour, and Ottawa in the winter during hockey season when she's not on the road. The singer says Fisher has friends in Nashville whom he met before the two started dating, so he feels right at home in Music City U.S.A. The pair have contracted to build a home in West Carleton, just a short distance from Scotiabank Place, where the Ottawa Senators are based, according to the *Ottawa Citizen*. Brian Howie is the builder and while he would not give out specific plans to reporters, he said it will be a very tasteful home that both Underwood and Fisher have helped design. The *Citizen* reports that it will be a 5,000 square foot brick-stone home.[42]

In her four-plus years of being in the celebrity spotlight, Underwood has managed to keep a clean-cut image despite rumors and speculation about her life as one of country music's newest singing sensations. At the same time, she's kept her career moving forward with songs her fans love and a live show that continues to fill venues around the country. In retrospect, she says much of it has been a blur. In a bio for her album *Carnival Ride*, Underwood said, "I remember certain things—'Saturday Night Live' was really cool," she says. "It was great to be added to the list of such great iconic artists who have performed on the show before. And of course, being on stage at the Grammys—that was an amazing moment. Who'd have thought? But each one runs together. I'd love to revel in the moment a little more sometimes."[43]

NOTES

1. Matt Elliott, "Carrie Nation," *Tulsa World*, November 17, 2006.

2. *CMT Insider*, http://www.cmt.com/shows/dyn/cmt_insider/113 097/episode.jhtml, December 9, 2006.

3. Ibid.

4. Vernell Hackett, Carrie Underwood Interview, Westwood One, October 2, 2007.

5. Ibid.

6. Ibid.

7. Ibid.

8. "Carrie Underwood: What She Eats for Clear Skin and 12 Other Secrets," *Self* magazine, January 2010.

9. Vernell Hackett, Carrie Underwood Interview, Westwood One, October 2, 2007.

10. Ibid.

11. Jennifer Chancellor, "Slide Show," *Tulsa World*, August 29, 2009.

12. Ibid.

13. Ibid.

14. Carrie Underwood Bio, *Great American Country*, www.gactv. com/gac/ar_az_carrie_underwood.

15. "Country Cares Seminar," *YouTube*, http://www.youtube.com/ watch?v=UNJFkuKwsbs, January 15, 2010.

16. "Carrie Underwood, Danny Gokey visit St. Jude Kids," *USA Today*, January 16, 2010.

17. Carrie In Badgley Mischka Campaign, http://www.carrieunder-woodofficial.com/news/carrie-in-badgley-mischka-campaign, March 3, 2009.

18. Alexandra Jacobs, "Finding Her Voice," *Allure*, April, 2010.

19. Claire Conners, "How I Lost 20 Pounds," *Shape*, February 2008.

20. Ibid.

21. Dave Karger, "Carrie Underwood and Tony Romo: A Passing Fancy," *Entertainment Weekly*, www.ew.com/…/0,,20007164_20008 533_20152859,00.html, October 17, 2007.

22. Ibid.

23. Tom Junod, "Carrie Underwood: What I've Learned," http://www. esquire.com/features/what-ive-learned/new-carrie-underwood-inter view-0110, December 9, 2009.

24. Tim Nudd, "Carrie Underwood 'Couldn't Imagine' Being Married Now," *People* magazine, http://www.people.com/people/article/0,,20152 995_20350143,00.html, October 18, 2007.

25. David Caplan and Charlotte Triggs, "Carrie Underwood on Chace Crawford: He's Really Cute," *People* magazine, http://www.peo ple.com/people/article/0,,20152766,00.html, October 17, 2007.

26. "Carrie's Texted Breakup with Chase," http://extratv.warnerbros.com/2008/04/carries_texted_breakup_with_ch.php, April 7, 2008.

27. Ibid.

28. "Mike Fisher: No Seranades for Carrie Underwood," *People* magazine, http://www.people.com/people/article/0,,20314444,00.html, March 3, 2009.

29. Ibid.

30. *Ellen DeGeneres Show,* November 18, 2009.

31. Jennifer Chancellor, "Carrie Underwood and Beau Get Engaged," *Tulsa World,* December 22, 2009.

32. "Carrie Underwood Gets Engaged!," *People* magazine, http://www.people.com/people/article/0,,20332166,00.html, December 21, 2009.

33. *Grecosize,* http://www.grecoleanandfit.com/, January 2, 2010.

34. Alexandra Jacobs, "Finding Her Voice," *Allure,* April 2010.

35. Eileen Finan, "Inside Carrie Underwood's Sparkly Southern Wedding!," http://www.people.com/people/article/0,,20401609,00.html, July 14, 2010.

36. Ibid.

37. Ibid.

38. Carrie Underwood Provides Details of Her Dream Wedding, http://thecelebritycafe.com/feature/carrie-underwood-provides-details-her-dream-wedding-07-14-2010, July 14, 2010.

39. Pernilla Cedenheim, "How Carrie Underwood is Spending Her Honeymoon," http://www.people.com/people/article/0,,20402877,00.html, July 18, 2010.

40. Denis Armstrong, "Carrie Underwood: Queen of Two Capitals," *Edmonton Sun,* QMI Agency, March 10, 2010.

41. Ibid.

42. Tony Lofaro, "Carrie Underwood, Mike Fisher Build House near Ottawa," the *Ottawa Citizen,* April 22, 2010.

43. Carrie Underwood Bio, Biography/www.carrieunderwoodofficial.com.

Chapter 7

CARNIVAL RIDE

There is much talk about the sophomore jinx for recording artists. As the saying goes, a singer has a lifetime to prepare for their first album and maybe a year to record the second one. Underwood was under a lot of pressure when she recorded *Some Hearts*, her first album release. That album was such a success, even Underwood had to wonder if her second project would be so popular. The singer was very much aware that people in the industry were wondering the same thing about her second CD. Even though she was rushed to record *Some Hearts*, traveling back and forth to Nashville to find songs and go in the studio during her 40-city "Pop Tarts Presents American Idols Live! Tour 2005," she had the momentum from her *Idol* win to achieve record sales of more than seven million albums. Fans who faithfully followed her during her weeks of competition were anxiously awaiting that first commercial CD. The question as she started to record the sophomore effort was, were they also anxious to buy her second album?

The relative newcomer to country music admits that as she entered the recording process for *Carnival Ride*, she couldn't help but think "Is there really anywhere to go but down?" Once she started to write and choose songs, she knew that was an unreasonable fear. "I realized it was more about making an album for myself that I love and I know I have a huge hand in making. Whatever happens, it's icing on the cake," she told *Billboard* magazine.[1]

One of the things Underwood was determined to do was write more songs for her next project. From the beginning, Underwood had said she hoped to become a songwriter, but she didn't know if she had the talent to do so. To her credit, she threw herself into the creative process and soaked up as much as she could from the writers that she worked with. Coming up with ideas and completing songs that would ultimately be chosen as part of her sophomore project helped the singer to grow in her confidence as a songwriter. She realized that she could pen the tunes that would ultimately shape her career and at the same time create a legacy through the songs she wrote.

In February 2007, she and a group of songwriters gathered at the Ryman Auditorium in Nashville, former home of the Grand Ole Opry, to work for several days in order to write songs for the new CD. Underwood and her management team brought together a great group of Nashville's finest tunesmiths for the songwriting retreat, including Brett James, Luke Laird, Kelley Lovelace, Aimee Mayo, and Steve McEwan. Some of these songwriters had contributed tunes to her first album; others were newcomers that Underwood really did not know. The purpose of the retreat was to write the best songs they could for Underwood's upcoming album. Not all songs would be chosen, but the purpose for the gathering was to write songs with Underwood to allow her to have a voice on her second release. She hoped to have a more personal album and one that was a direct reflection of her thoughts and feelings, which was the main reason to get with the group of songwriters.

"They're incredibly talented, but even they need direction sometimes," Underwood explained in an interview for *American Way* magazine. "It's not fair to say, 'Hey, Carrie Underwood is working on a new album, so write for her.' They don't know me personally; they don't know what direction I want to take the album. It was important to all of us to get together so I could hang out with them. And we started writing, and soon we had all these great songs. . . . It was awesome."[2]

The singer worked with the various songwriters to craft tunes that reflected where she was at the time she was recording her second album. Much had changed in the couple of years that Underwood had been in the limelight, growing from a competitor on a national television show, to a competitor in the international business of country music. The young college student who tried out for *American Idol* had become an award-winning country music star, and much more is expected from that type celebrity than the person she was when she recorded her first album. One of the problems Underwood encountered in looking for songs was that it seemed hard to find writers that understood young female artists. She was 22 when she won *American Idol*, and just a year and a half later she was looking for another set of songs. "There are all these male writers and they are great at what they do," she told *Billboard*. "But I'm a 24-year-old girl, and I imagine it would be hard for these guys to think like a 24-year-old girl. So it's really awesome that I've been able to get together with someone like Hillary Lindsey, who is one of my favorite writers."[3]

When the retreat was over and Underwood had a chance to go back through the songs that she and the other writers had written, she was very pleased with what she had. The group of writers had come up with multiple songs for the singer to choose from for the new album and she felt that they had set the bar high as far as the caliber of songs that eventually ended up on the new disc. Underwood didn't want to venture too far from her original roots with her second album. Just as with *Some Hearts*, the singer decided to stay with the country sound that brought her to the limelight. Late in 2006, she told the *Tulsa World* that people continually ask her if she plans a different direction for her sophomore album. "I definitely want to stick to country and just get great songs once again, and, you know, try to get the people what they seem to like." She also indicated a willingness to move around within the genre, explaining that some of her work might be traditional country, while other songs might be more pop. She stresses, however, that she has no desire to cross over into other genres unless it just happens with one of her country hits.[4]

Even though she's a new artist, Underwood says she has the opportunity to state her opinion in every aspect of her career. "I have a say in everything," Underwood said. "Like, I think people think that other people just tell me what to do. Fortunately, I work with some really awesome people. Everything gets run by me first."[5]

This was definitely true when Underwood went in to record what would become her second album, *Carnival Ride*. Once she and her team picked the songs to record, the singer went into the studio to start the recording process. "We really took the first part of the year to make sure we had the best material we could possibly find," she explains, "and then we went in every day to the studio, which is something I really love to do. It is a very controlled environment. My producer, Mark Bright, is so easy to work with. He'll encourage me to play around with vocal approaches because, at the end of the day, it's my voice, and the song is something I'll be doing on stage every night. He trusts the instincts I have and I trust him. That makes us a good team."[6]

Underwood says she could hear a lot of growth in her voice over the past couple of years since she recorded the debut album, not the least of which was the fact that she was able to hit some notes she couldn't hit before. "I think I sound different now," she told *Entertainment Weekly*. "I've gotten a lot more practice and everything's just gotten easier. Like, notes that I could barely hit for the first album—like, 'Oh my gosh, this is gonna kill me'—are a piece of cake now. We're on to new notes now that are way in the stratosphere. On "All-American Girl," the high note is the highest I've ever hit."[7]

If *Some Hearts* captured the innocence of a young woman emerging on the biggest adventure of her life, *Carnival Ride* set out to show her fans the journey she had traveled and how she had emerged as a stronger artist and woman than she had been at the beginning of the ride to international stardom. Underwood showed remarkable progress with her vocals, despite the fact that her voice was strong throughout the *Idol* competition. She also stepped up to the plate as far as her songwriting, penning four of the songs for the project. Not the least of Underwood's changes was her growth as an artist and in her personal life. Someone who comes from a farming community in Oklahoma to walk red carpets in Nashville, Los Angeles, Las Vegas, and New York must find a way to cope with their new-found situation as quickly as possible. Despite having a somewhat shy personality, Underwood learned quickly that she had to overcome any inhibitions of being around people to mix and mingle with industry VIPs as well as other celebrities of all ranks, from peers Taylor Swift, Chris Daughtry, David Cook, and Miranda Lambert to superstars Dolly Parton and Reba McEntire, hip-hop singer Eve, actress Teri Hatcher of *Desperate Housewives,* and rock star/musician Slash.

In her record company's bio sheet for *Carnival Ride*, Underwood talks about her mindset going into recording the album. "Last time, I didn't set out to talk about a specific thing. I just picked songs that reminded me of home and made me think, 'Wow! I can relate to that,' and by the end, there was a theme." This time, Underwood says, she drew on her instincts as a fan in selecting songs that range from the enchantingly light-hearted to the deeply inspiring. She approached the album with the idea that it would be a collection of songs people would want to hear on the radio, and as the cowriter on several of them, songs that would give her fans a little more insight into who she is. Several of the songs did indeed give fans insight into Underwood's life and personality. The single, "All-American Girl," which Underwood cowrote with Ashley Gorley and Kelley Lovelace, is the story of a little girl born into a household where the father really wants a boy. The accompanying video explains just how quickly the father changes his mind when he sees that baby girl for the first time and watches her grow up. Another song that sets a tone for the album is "Crazy Dreams," in which Underwood proclaims that "even crazy dreams come true," something she can sing with certainty. The tune was penned by Underwood, Troy Verges, and Barry G. Dean. The first single from the project, "So Small," cowritten with Hillary Lindsey and Luke Laird, is a song about the important things in life, along the line of the phrase, "Don't sweat the small stuff." The fourth song she wrote, "Last Name," cowritten with Hillary, is a fun song that shows the lighter side of Underwood's personality.

Lindsey, who cowrote Underwood's first major country hit, "Jesus, Take the Wheel," has become good friends with the singer. The two first met during the time Underwood was choosing songs for her debut album, when the record label put the singer and a group of songwriters together at a songwriter retreat in Nashville after Underwood won *American Idol*. The purpose of that retreat was to select songs for *Some Hearts*. As she got to know Underwood better, Lindsey consequently penned several other tunes that fit into the concept of the second album, specifically "Wheel Of the World," "Get Out of This Town," "Twisted," and "Just a Dream." The latter became a powerful single and video for the singer.

Another song, "I Told You So," was a cover of a tune that had been a hit for Randy Travis in 1988. Underwood and Randy did a duet of the song, which was released as a single and also a digital download. Underwood says she had loved Randy ever since she was a little girl, and meeting him was a breathtaking experience for her. "When I first met Randy

Travis, it was a definite moment," Carrie revealed to Jeff Foxworthy on his radio show. "I felt so bad because I went up, and I met him, and you know that's somebody I've known since birth, so to get to meet him and to get to hang out with him and stuff like that, I just started telling him how important he was—as if he didn't know—to so many people. And I got all teary-eyed, and [said], 'I'm so sorry I'm that girl now!' He was so good with me."[8]

Carnival Ride has sold more than three million copies. Released October 23, 2007, and produced by Mark Bright, the CD debuted at the top of Billboard's Top Country Albums and the Billboard 200 all-genre chart, bolstered by first-week sales of 527,101. At the time of its release, the title earned the highest first-week sales figures for any female artist in any genre. It also garnered the biggest country debut in digital album chart history, with digital sales of 44,928. Underwood was named Billboard 200 Top Selling Female Artist of 2007.

The record label released a total of five singles from Carnival Ride. Her first single, "So Small," was released August 28, 2007. It stayed number one on Billboard's country singles chart for three weeks. The tune entered the country airplay chart at 20, making it the highest chart entry by a solo country female in the Nielsen BDS (Broadcast Data Systems) history. It was certified Gold for 500,000 digital downloads by the Recording Industry Association of America (RIAA), and Underwood was named the 2008 BMI Songwriter of the Year for her part in writing the tune. BMI (Broadcast Music Inc.) is a performing rights organization that represents songwriters and collects their performance royalties for them. There are three such organizations—ASCAP (American Society of Composers, Authors and Publishers) and SESAC (Society of European Stage Authors & Composers) are the other two.

The second single, "All-American Girl," stayed two weeks at the top of Billboard's country single chart, and its accompanying video was the fastest rising video in the history of the CMT Network's Top 20 list. It was the top country music video, song, and music video on iTunes and was CMT's number one streamed music video. "All-American Girl" was Underwood's sixth consecutive number one and her second consecutive hit as a songwriter. It was released December 17, 2007. Underwood was honored with a BMI songwriter award for the song, and it was named ASCAP's Most Played Country Song of the Year. The single was certified by RIAA for the sale of 500,000 downloads.

The third single, "Last Name," released April 7, 2008, only stayed at number one for a week, but it was enough to make Underwood the only artist in country chart history to have their first seven country singles all reach the top of the charts. It won a 2009 Grammy for Best Country Female Performance, and the tune was the 2009 People's Choice for Favorite Country Song. It also earned her recognition from the RIAA for 500,000 purchased downloads.

Underwood further boosted her status in country music by taking home Female Vocalist at the Academy of Country Music Awards in Las Vegas on May 18, 2008. "I know I don't deserve it, but I'll take it," she said as she accepted the award. She went on to thank her fans, telling them, "Fans got me everything I have, and I owe everything to you." She opened the show performing "Last Name." Underwood also did a tribute to the late Eddy Arnold, a member of the Country Music Hall of Fame who had just passed away. She and friend Brad Paisley performed "Make the World Go Away," one of Arnold's classic hits.

"Just A Dream," released July 24, 2008, was Underwood's fourth single off *Carnival Ride*. The tune stayed at the top of the *Billboard* country singles chart for two weeks, extending her run of number one singles to eight. It was nominated for the Academy of Country Music's Video of the Year and once again certified as a Gold single by the RIAA for 500,000 digital downloads.

Underwood's fifth single, released on February 2, 2009, was a remake of Randy Travis's "I Told You So." The single also shot to the top of *Billboard*'s country singles chart. The song made the singer the first country artist to achieve 10 number one singles off of their first two album releases. Underwood became the first country artist to take a remake of a previously released song to number one since Alan Jackson's 2000 success with "It Must Be Love," originally released by Don Williams. "I Told You So" was also certified a Gold single by the RIAA, with sales of 500,000 copies.

Carnival Ride turned out to be a huge success for Underwood and has taken her on a journey she never dared to dream about when she was on her way to that first *American Idol* competition in St. Louis, Missouri. The singer says her favorite metaphor for the journey actually comes from a song on the album. Written by Hillary Lindsey, Chris Lindsey, and Aimee Mayo, the song "Wheel of the World" states that God put us on this carnival ride of life and we never know where the ride will take us.

"This part of my life has been absolutely crazy," Underwood says, "and to think it all started from one little decision I made to get on that ride. That's why 'Carnival Ride' works as my album title, because it describes the wonderful craziness I've been through over the past couple of years."

The popularity of *Carnival Ride* offered other opportunities to Underwood. She joined Brad Paisley for a song on his album *5th Gear,* singing "Oh Love" with her former tour mate. She also recorded an original song for the Disney movie *Enchanted.* Her rendition of "Ever Ever After" resulted in a music video for the project. On Jan 20, 2008, Underwood joined some of country music's top artists to tape "How Great Thou Art: Gospel Favorites Live from the Grand Ole Opry." The artists, among them Trace Adkins, Dierks Bentley, Charlie Daniels, Sara Evans, Vince Gill, Patty Loveless, Loretta Lynn, Ronnie Milsap, and Ricky Skaggs, performed some of their favorite gospel tunes while performing on the *Grand Ole Opry.* Later the live performances were packaged into an album by the same name and released by RCA.

Underwood made the prestigious Forbes list, Cash Queens of Music, consisting of the top-earning entertainers from June 2006 to June 2007, when it was released on January 29, 2008. She was listed at number 15, with gross earnings in 2007 of $7 million. That's pretty good for a young lady who had only been in the country music business for two years! Ahead of her was Faith Hill, at eight with $19 million; the Dixie Chicks at nine with $18 million; and Martina McBride at 13 with $12 million. Topping the list was Madonna, who earned $72 million. Barbra Streisand was in the second spot, earning $60 million. Criteria for the income used to compile the list included concert grosses, merchandising revenue, album sales, and additional revenue streams from ancillary businesses such as clothing lines, fragrance deals, and endorsements.

The singer continued to receive awards throughout 2008 and 2009. During the 50th annual Grammy presentation on February 10, 2008, she was awarded Best Female Country Vocal Performance for "Before He Cheats," and songwriters Josh Kear and Chris Tompkins received nods for Best Country Song.

On February 23, 2008, Underwood made her second appearance on NBC's *Saturday Night Live.* She sang "All-American Girl" on the episode, which was hosted by Tina Fey. Steve Martin made a surprise appearance on the show.

Early in 2009 she was named Best Country Female Vocal Performance for "Last Name" at the Grammys. In May of that year she was named the Academy of Country Music's Entertainer of the Year, making her only the seventh woman in the history of the show's 42 years to take home that award. At the same time she was named the Academy's Female Vocalist of the Year.

One of the most important things the hit album did for Underwood was pair her with Keith Urban for a tour in early 2007. The Urban-Underwood tour was titled "Love, Pain & the Whole Crazy Carnival Ride Tour." It kicked off January 31, 2008 in Uncasville, Connecticut, for a 24-city trek that ended in Lexington, Kentucky, on April 26. The tour name was derived from each of the artist's two albums: Keith's double Platinum "Love, Pain & the Whole Crazy Thing" and Underwood's "Carnival Ride."

In a press release issued jointly by their publicists, Keith said of the tour, "I'm looking forward to hitting the road with Underwood and to bringing our audiences together for what I think will be a magical night of sights, sounds, songs and solos." Underwood agreed, adding, "I can't think of a better person to begin 2008 with than Keith. He is an amazing entertainer and a well-respected musician, singer and songwriter."

"Love, Pain & the Whole Crazy Carnival Ride Tour"
with Keith Urban and Carrie Underwood:

January 31   Uncasville, CT (Mohegan Sun Arena)

February 1   Uncasville, CT (Mohegan Sun Arena)

February 2   Rochester, NY (Blue Cross Arena)

February 13   New York, NY (Madison Square Garden)

February 14   Hershey, PA (Giant Center)

February 15   Atlantic City, NJ (Boardwalk Hall)

February 16   Roanoke, VA (Roanoke Civic Center)

February 29   Tallahassee, FL (Leon County Civic Center)

March 1   Biloxi, MS (Mississippi Coast Coliseum)

March 5   Kansas City, MO (Sprint Center)

March 6   Wichita, KS (Kansas Coliseum)

March 7   Omaha, NE (Qwest Center)

March 8   Denver, CO (Pepsi Center)

March 11   San Jose, CA (HP Pavillion)

March 12   Sacramento, CA (Arco Arena)

March 13   Anaheim, CA (Honda Center)

April 9   Baltimore, MD (1st Mariner Arena)

April 10   Charlottesville, VA (John Paul Jones Arena)

April 11   Charleston, WV (Charleston Civic Center)

April 12   State College, PA (Bryce Jordan Center)

April 17   Charleston, SC (North Charleston Coliseum)

April 18   Charlotte, NC (Bobcat Arena)

April 19   Raleigh, NC (RBC Center)

April 22   Peoria, IL (Peoria Civic Center Arena)

April 24   Gwinnett, GA (Gwinnett Center)

April 25   Gwinnett, GA (Gwinnett Center)

April 26   Lexington, KY (Rupp Arena)

In February 2008, just as Underwood was hitting the road with Keith Urban on their joint tour, she announced that she would be headlining her own tour later in the year. Dubbed "The Carnival Ride Tour," it kicked off on May 2 in Tucson, Arizona. The singer continued adding dates for her debut as a headliner until it went through December 14. Special guests on varying segments of the tour were Josh Turner, Jason Michael Carroll, and Little Big Town. Underwood was delighted but nervous about stepping out on her first headline tour.

"I'm so excited to be hitting the road and doing the full show of my music that I have always dreamt of doing," Underwood said in a press release issued by her record label. "I have been so fortunate to learn from so many other great artists while touring with them, and they have inspired me in so many ways. They have helped me to get to this stage of my first real headline shows, and now I finally feel ready. I can't wait to travel throughout the U.S. and Canada and see all my fans."[9]

When an artist is an opening act for someone, the pressure is on the headliner more so than it is on the first or second person on the bill. Of course Underwood wanted to do well on all of her shows, whether it was with Brad Paisley or Keith Urban, for by doing so she would win more fans and be assured that she would be asked to be on another tour. In addition, the opening act is chosen in the hope that they will bring in some fans of their own that might not have bought tickets for the headliner's tour.

As a headliner, the pressure is really on the person whose name is at the top of the show bill. It is their responsibility to sell the majority of the tickets for each show, and they have to work to promote the tour by doing interviews with radio and newspapers in the area where the show is being held. Often the record label will do promotions with local radio, where they will give away albums or tickets to the show to help promote it and build excitement for the performance.

Another thing an artist tries to do is give their fans some one-on-one time with them. Underwood reached superstar status very quickly, so she was not able to sit at a table after the show and sign autographs for every fan who wanted to speak to her. At this point in a career, the artist works within their fan club roster, usually working out a system where they can see a certain number of fans in each city where they perform. They sometimes are asked to do special meet-and-greet sessions with winners from a local radio station as well, and occasionally people from their sponsor are at the show and expect to go backstage and say hello. From the front of the stage it all looks like glamour and excitement, but from the aspect of the artist, it's hard work, even though they love what they do.

When Underwood's "Carnival Ride Tour," sponsored by Vitamin Water, wrapped in mid-December 2008, she had played before nearly 1.2 million people. One of the places she performed was Tulsa, Oklahoma, near her hometown of Checotah. The singer told the *Tulsa World* that she was excited to be coming home to perform. "It's been awhile. It's been too long, and I'm very excited to play Tulsa and the new BOK

Center. Hometown crowds are always so great. I'm looking forward, because a lot of my friends and family are going to be there. It's home."[10]

Carrie Underwood "Carnival Ride Tour"

May 2	Tucson, AZ (Tucson Convention Center)
May 6	El Paso, TX (Don Haskins Center)
May 11	North Little Rock, AR (Alltel Arena)
May 19	Reno, NV (Reno Events Center)
May 25	Nampa, ID (Idaho Center)
May 28	Fresno, CA (Save Mart Center)
June 8	Cape Girardeau, MO (Show Me Center)
June 10	Toledo, OH (Seagate Center)
June 12	Reading, PA (Sovereign Center)
June 14	Huntington, WV (Big Sandy Superstore Arena)
June 15	Greenville, SC (BI-LO Center)
June 18	Lafayette, LA (Cajundome)
June 20	Mobile, AL (Mobile Civic Center)
June 21	Beaumont, TX (Ford Park)
June 22	Corpus Christi, TX (American Bank Center)
June 24	New Orleans, LA (Lakefront Arena)
July 16	Twin Lakes, WI (Country Thunder USA)
July 19	Eau Claire, WI (Country Jam USA)
July 21	Harrington, DE (Delaware State Fair)
July 26	Kelseyville, CA (Konocti Harbor Resort)
August 1	Mashantucket, CT (Foxwoods Resort Casino)
August 2	Toms River Township, NJ (Toms River Fest)
August 8	Indianapolis, IN (Indiana State Fair)

September 19   Puyallup, WA (Puyallup Fair)

September 23   Cleveland, OH (Wolstein Center)

September 24   Highland Heights, KY (The Bank of Kentucky Center)

September 25   Milwaukee, WI (Bradley Center)

September 27   Grand Forks, ND (Ralph Engelstad Arena)

September 28   Sioux City, IA (Gateway Arena)

September 30   Topeka, KS (Landon Arena)

October 2   Champaign, IL (Assembly Hall)

October 3   Hoffman Estates, IL (Sears Centre)

October 4   Detroit, MI (Joe Louis Arena)

October 6   London, Ontario, Canada (John Labatt Centre)

October 7   Toronto, Ontario, Canada (Air Canada Centre)

October 10   Saint John, New Brunswick, Canada (Harbour Station)

October 11   Moncton, New Brunswick, Canada (Moncton Coliseum)

October 12   Halifax, Nova Scotia, Canada (Halifax Metro Centre)

October 14   Portland, ME (Cumberland County Civic Center)

October 15   Boston, MA (Agganis Arena)

October 16   Kingston, RI (Ryan Center)

October 18   Syracuse, NY (War Memorial at Oncenter)

October 19   Philadelphia, PA (Liacouras Center)

October 21   Newark, NJ (Prudential Center)

October 23   Hampton, VA (Hampton Coliseum)

October 24   Winston-Salem, NC (Lawrence Joel Veterans Memorial Coliseum)

October 26	Southaven, MS (DeSoto Civic Center)
October 27	Jonesboro, AR (Convocation Center ASU)
October 29	Tulsa, OK (BOK Center)
October 30	Grand Prairie, TX (Nokia Theatre at Grand Prairie)
November 1	Houston, TX (Reliant Arena)
November 2	San Antonio, TX (AT&T Center)
November 5	Los Angeles, CA (Nokia Theatre)
November 6	Las Cruces, NM (Pan American Center)
November 7	Glendale, AZ (Jobing.com Arena)
November 8	San Diego, CA (San Diego Sports Arena)
November 9	Ontario, CA (Citizens Business Bank Arena)
November 14	Bakersfield, CA (Rabobank Arena)
November 15	Oakland, CA (Oracle Arena)
November 17	Portland, OR (Rose Garden Arena)
November 19	West Valley City, UT (E Center)
November 21	Missoula, MT (Adams Center)
November 22	Billings, MT (Rimrock Auto Arena at MetraPark)
November 24	Lethbridge, Alberta, Canada (ENMAX Centre)
November 25	Edmonton, Alberta, Canada (Rexall Place)
November 29	Saskatoon, Saskatchewan, Canada (Credit Union Centre)
December 1	Winnipeg, Manitoba, Canada (MTS Centre)
December 2	Madison, WI (Alliant Energy Center)
December 5	St. Louis, MI (Cheifetz Arena)
December 7	Nashville, TN (Sommet Center)
December 8	Chattanooga, TN (McKenzie Arena)
December 9	Tupelo, MS (BancorpSouth Arena)

December 12   Tampa, FL (St. Pete Times Forum)

December 13   Orlando, FL (UCF Arena)

December 14   Gainesville, Florida (Stephen C. O'Connell Center)

Underwood not only performed her hits on the "Carnival Ride" tour, she delved into songs from her albums that had not been hits for her to help round out the performances for her fans. The basic set list for the tour was:

"Flat on the Floor"
"Wasted"
"Get Out of This Town"
"The More Boys I Meet"
"Just a Dream"
"Jesus, Take the Wheel"
"I Know You Won't"
"I Ain't in Checotah Anymore"
"Crazy Dreams"
"I Told You So"
"Some Hearts" medley ("Lessons Learned," "That's Where It Is,"
    "We're Young & Beautiful," "Some Hearts")
"Last Name"
"Don't Forget to Remember Me"
"Twisted"
"All-American Girl"
"So Small"

Encore:
"November Rain"
"Paradise City"
"Before He Cheats"

In the midst of her tour, Underwood accepted another challenge. Together with friend Brad Paisley, who was one of the first entertainers to invite her to go on tour, she cohosted the CMA Awards on November 12, 2008. "Brad and I are really good friends and I can't think of anyone that I'd rather be hanging out with on stage than him," Underwood told the *Tulsa World*. "I know we're going to do a really good job, but I am really nervous because neither one of us have really done anything like this before."

Underwood was thrilled that the CMA had offered her the opportunity to step outside the norm and take on cohosting duties. "I am so excited to host a show I grew up watching, and am so thrilled to spend this night with the fans and Brad," she said. "It's going to be a party!" The singer was nominated for Female Vocalist of the Year, which she had won the previous year, and had a first-time nod for Album of the Year for *Carnival Ride*.[11]

Underwood was certainly familiar with the CMA Awards show, as she had already won Female Vocalist in 2006 and 2007, the Horizon award in 2006, and Single of the Year for "Before He Cheats" in 2007. In 2008 she was nominated in the Female Vocalist of the Year and Best Album categories. She not only did an outstanding job as cohost, she maintained her title as CMA's Female Vocalist for the third year in a row.

Carrie Underwood accepts the Female Vocalist of the Year award during the 42nd Annual CMA Awards show on Nov. 12, 2008, in Nashville, Tennessee. (AP Photo/Darron Cummings.)

While the singer admits she doesn't keep count of her awards, she does have a special place for them. Underwood says she keeps the various awards at her home but not on prominent display because she considers her home a sanctuary where she can go and get away from the business of music for a while. Underwood ended 2008 and began 2009 with awards. On Nov 23, 2008, she took home the Favorite Country Album honor for *Carnival Ride* at the American Music Awards. Then she started the new year in a big way at the 35th annual People's Choice Awards on January 7, 2009, taking home two trophies—Favorite Female Singer and Favorite Country Song for "Last Name." A month later, Underwood continued her Grammy wins, receiving the Best Female Country Vocal Performance for "Last Name" at the 51st annual Grammy awards in Los Angeles.

On March 18, Underwood took one of her idols, Randy Travis, to Fox's *American Idol* to sing his original hit, "I Told You So." Brad Paisley also guested on that segment of *Idol*, performing "Then," a love song to his wife. Three weeks later, on April 5, she was in Las Vegas, picking up Entertainer of the Year and Top Female Vocalist honors at the 44th annual Academy of Country Music Awards show at the MGM Grand. She created quite a sensation with the deep red merlot silk taffeta dress she wore at the awards show. Designed by Rafael Cennamo of Miami, Florida, the dress took 120 yards of fabric and had an eight-foot train. "It was such an honor to wear such a beautiful dress during one of the most special nights of my life," said Underwood, who performed her hit "I Told You So" during the show.

Country music expanded its horizons to a bigger audience when Underwood won *American Idol*. It also expanded when former lead singer for Hootie & the Blowfish, Darius Rucker, recorded a country album that did very well for him. On April 5, Oprah Winfrey invited Rucker, Underwood, Kenny Chesney, and Sugarland to join her on a special country edition of *The Oprah Winfrey Show*. That segment also did a lot to expand country music's exposure to an even wider audience.

Underwood caught the attention of *Forbes* magazine again, this time making its Celebrity 100 power list on June 3, 2009. She came in at number 75, while Kenny Chesney showed at 31, Miley Cyrus at 29, Rascal Flatts at 42, Toby Keith at 59, and Taylor Swift at 69. An even higher honor was bestowed on Underwood on June 11, 2009, when the exhibit

"Carrie Underwood: All-American Girl" opened at the Country Music Hall of Fame and Museum in Nashville. Among items fans can see is the merlot red silk taffeta dress worn at the Academy of Country Music Awards in 2009.

Underwood continued to receive honors throughout 2009. On September 17, she was inducted into the Oklahoma Music Hall of Fame during ceremonies at the Muskogee Civic Center. Also inducted that evening were Ramona Reed, the only female to record a duet with Bob Wills, and musician Rocky Frisco. They joined other Hall of Fame alumni Ronnie Dunn of Brooks & Dunn, Vince Gill, Toby Keith, and Leon Russell. Later in the year, Underwood donated lyric and music sheets from her hit single, "I Ain't in Checotah Anymore," to the Hall of Fame.

On November 11, 2009, Underwood joined friend Brad Paisley as repeat hosts of the CMA Awards in Nashville. She did a great job of cohosting the CBS special, appearing much more relaxed than the first time she hosted the event in 2008.

Underwood's new hometown, Nashville, honored her on December 12 with the Harmony Award during ceremonies at the annual Symphony Ball, held at the Schermerhorn Symphony Hall. It is given to individuals who have demonstrated continued interest in and support of music in Nashville, have exemplified the connections between the diverse music of the city, and have contributed to the development and appreciation of music culture. Others who have been honored with the award include Dolly Parton, Trisha Yearwood, Amy Grant, Chet Atkins, and the Judds. "I feel like I'm getting more involved in Nashville," Underwood told the crowd gathered to honor her. "I'm going to be here for a very long time, if not for the rest of my life, and I love it here, so it's nice to feel like I'm part of this town."[12]

NOTES

1. Deborah Evans Price, "Country Star Underwood Enjoys Fast-Moving 'Ride,'" *Billboard*, September 6, 2007.

2. Eric Celeste, "Carried Away," *American Way*, September 1, 2008.

3. Price, "Country Star Underwood."

4. Matt Elliott, "Carrie Nation," *Tulsa World*, November 17, 2006.

5. Ibid.

6. Ibid.

7. Dave Karger, "Carrie Underwood: A Very Private Idol Speaks Out," *Entertainment Weekly*, October 26, 2007.

8. Pat Gallagher, "Carrie Underwood Was 'That Girl' Meeting Randy Travis," *The Boot*, http://www.theboot.com/2009/12/02/carrie-underwood-randy-travis/, December 2, 2009.

9. "Carrie Underwood Embarks on 'Carnival Ride' Tour in May," Press Release Issued by Sony Nashville Records.

10. Staff Reports, "Carrie Underwood, Brad Paisley to host CMA Awards," *Tulsa World*, October 10, 2009.

11. Ibid.

12. Carrie Underwood, Speech at Presentation of Harmony Award on December 12, 2009, Schemerhorn Symphony Hall, Nashville, Tennessee.

Chapter 8

SONGS LIKE THIS

When Underwood arrived in Nashville to record her first album she did not know how the music business worked, but she was determined to learn as much about her new career as quickly as she could. One of the things she decided very quickly was that she would like to learn to write songs. Although she did do a little writing for *Some Hearts*, it wasn't until her second album, *Carnival Ride*, that she really started to make statements as a songwriter.

Underwood totally immersed herself in the writing and recording of her second disc. She told Westwood One Radio that the best part of making that album was that she was more involved in general as well as being part of the writing process for the album. "That was a really good learning experience for me and it was really fun. I think everybody did such a fantastic job at every level, and having that finished product in your hand is just an amazing feeling. The whole thought process mainly was just about doing the best job that we could."[1] She also said that she was more pleased with the second project because she did have so much input into the writing and recording process. "I think there's a lot more of me on it so I personally am a lot more satisfied with this album than the first one in musical terms and the songs on it."[2]

When Underwood was listening to songs for her first album, the team around her came up with the idea of holding a writer's retreat, where various songwriters who were at the top of their game in Nashville could come together to meet the singer, get to know her a little bit, and pitch songs they had or write new ones for her. At the time, Underwood wasn't involved in the writing of the songs very much. By the time the second album rolled around, she was ready to jump into the fray and try her hand at writing tunes for the upcoming project.

Since the first writer's retreat had worked well in coming up with tunes for *Some Hearts*, everyone agreed to do a second one to see what might come out of it. Organizers brought together a group of songwriters, some who already knew Underwood and some who did not, setting up the retreat at the Ryman Auditorium in Nashville in February 2007. The Ryman is the former home of the Grand Ole Opry, and as such welcomed country music greats including Hank Williams, Dottie West, Bill Monroe, Earl Scruggs, Lester Flatt, Bill Anderson, Vince Gill, and Marty Stuart to its stage over the years. Perhaps the management team thought the vibes from these great entertainers and songwriters would lend a creative aura to the retreat.

Underwood recalled the setup for the retreat for Westwood One. "Well, there were about a dozen writers there and a lot of them I had worked with before. We did have some people there that I had never worked with before so it was a really good setting for me to get together with these writers I really didn't necessarily know so well so there was a lot less pressure I think. It was a big group of us and different people split up into different groups for the day and hung out and wrote. Then they would switch partners or team up with somebody else and write with them for awhile."[3]

While "anything goes" was the motto for the retreat, the bottom line was to write 15 to 20 great songs for Underwood to consider recording for the album. It was understood that every song written during this time would not necessarily be recorded for the album, but it was also understood that Underwood was definitely interested in having some of the songs she cowrote included on the final disc.

Among the reasons that Underwood wanted to contribute songs she had a hand in writing for the sophomore album was the personal aspect it would bring to the project. "I think things just naturally end up being more personal and more believable if you have a hand in their creation," she told Westwood One. "I mean if you can get in there and write things in a song the way you would say them or the way you think about them, it's just much more believable. When you're on stage. you're singing something that you believed in so much that you sat down and wrote it down on a piece of paper."[4]

Underwood also acknowledged that she did not know if she had the talent to make it in the songwriting community. "I definitely knew that I might not be a good writer so when I when I went into the retreat it was to learn. I knew I would be learning from the best because the writers who were at the retreat were all really talented, plus they were really genuinely nice people and fun to hang out. Every day was fun we just went in to see what we could do, and if nothing else I learned something."[5]

Underwood also says she was aware that the things she wrote might not be good enough for the album. "I just wanted to see what I could do and if nothing came out of it, if I was the worst writer in the world, I would have been the first one to admit that and say 'Alright I'm going to leave it up to these people that actually know what they're doing to write the songs.' But if I could pull it off, it would just make things that much better. It would be more icing on the cake."[6]

The singer cowrote four songs that ended up on the album, but she says she honestly tried to pick the songs that were best for the project they were recording. "I never tried to push my own stuff or say that I wanted to have at least this many of my songs on the album. If one of my songs made it, that was great. If it didn't make it, that was okay too. I think there were some great songs that we wrote that didn't make the album but maybe other people didn't think they were so great. Either way I was very pleased with just getting in there and trying."[7]

When a singer does contribute to the songs on their album, it does indeed make the album more personal. In some cases with Underwood, the songs became autobiographical. "Crazy Dreams" is a good example of that. Underwood explained to Westwood One, "When we got in there and started writing that song I wanted to have an upbeat song. I love having songs that are happy for no reason, and something that if you're listening to it, maybe it can make your day a little bit better. That's the kind of the approach we took with 'Crazy Dreams'—just about how you might be coming up from behind but if you keep a good attitude and a positive attitude and you keep smiling through all of it, and you keep your free spirit going, then things really are possible. I am definitely a sterling example of how, if you keep believing that things really are possible, then anything could happen to you know. So yeah, it's definitely very autobiographical and it'll be fun to sing on stage cause I can mean every single word of it, you know."[8]

If "Crazy Dreams" was autobiographical, the single "So Small" validated Underwood's entry to a career as a songwriter in addition to her already established venture as a singer and entertainer. It was the first song she had a hand in writing that was chosen as a single. It went on to stay at the top of the *Billboard* country singles chart for three weeks and earned Underwood recognition as BMI's 2008 Songwriter of the Year for her part in writing the tune.

"I hope it's not a one time thing," Underwood said during a press conference at her number one party for "So Small." "I hope there's something else that I had a hand in writing that will also do well for me." Underwood acknowledged that she had written the song with some extremely talented people, and she knew some folks would be cynical enough to think that her name was just added to the song and she didn't really contribute to it all that much. "That's true, writing with Hillary Lindsey and Luke Laird is a great experience," Underwood admitted, adding, "Hopefully we can do it [have a hit with a song she's written] at least twice so that people can see that I'm really not bad at it [songwriting]."[9]

Underwood's wish definitely came true, as the next two songs from *Carnival Ride* that were released as singles were also tunes that she had a hand in writing. "Last Name" and "All-American Girl" both came from cowrites between Underwood and several other songwriters. While "Last Name" was a fun song that showed the side of Underwood that a lot of folks don't get to see, "All-American Girl" was once again autobiographical, in that it was about a man who wished for a son but rallied once his daughter was born. The girl in the tune becomes a little bit of everything, from an astronaut to a news anchorwoman, and her father is proud of whatever she decides to do. It too went to number one on *Billboard's* country singles chart, staying there for a two-week run.

Another reason to write your own songs, from an entertainer's viewpoint, is that they can visualize how the song will come off live and how fans will react to it. By the time the second album rolled around, Underwood had been in front of her fans enough to know what they liked at her live shows. Every artist wants to have a balance of up-tempo songs and a few great power ballads to make the evening entertaining for their audience. Not only was Underwood interested in having songs that came off well in a live concert setting, she wanted tunes that were catchy enough that her fans would be singing them back to her. There's nothing more satisfying for a songwriter than having a sold out house of 15,000 fans singing a song you wrote back to you! "You just know when you write a song when it's going to be so fun to sing and people are going to be out there singing it with me, and it's going to just rock out," Underwood told Westwood One.[10]

Underwood opened *Carnival Ride* with a song that she did not have a hand in writing, "Flat on the Floor." She told Westwood One that she wanted the first song on the project to be country, so it would set the tone for the album and let people know that she was a contemporary country singer. She added that she felt that the album definitely had a more contemporary country feel to it. "I just feel like if there were ever anybody that would try to say 'Oh Underwood's not country,' then this album should definitely prove something to those people. Not that I feel like I have anything to prove to those people, but it would do that."[11]

By the time Underwood's third album, *Play On*, was being recorded, she was much more confident in her ability as a songwriter. She cowrote seven of the 13 songs on the disc and says she revealed more about herself in this album than she has in previous ones. "I'm not an easy person to get to know, and I feel like I keep a lot of myself closed off to the world," she told *Billboard*. "It's really nice to be able to scratch the surface and to be able to open myself up a little more."[12]

Underwood also expanded her cowriting team to include a few songwriters from the pop and rock genre. In addition to working with Nashville writers Hillary Lindsey, Luke Laird, Brett James, and Gordie Sampson, she included BMI Pop Songwriter of the Year Kara DioGuardi, Mike Elizondo of Dr. Dre and Eminem fame, Raine Maida of the rock band Our Lady Peace, and his wife, Canadian songstress Chantal Kreviazuk.

"I listen to all kinds of music, all genres," Underwood told *Billboard*. "Bringing somebody from a different world into my world to see what their influence can do in my writing style—it's a lot of fun." Lest fans think she is getting ready to cross over, Underwood hastened to assure that she has no intention of switching out of the country genre. "I'm promising right now it would never happen."[13]

Underwood is a contemporary country singer. While she knows her country roots and is quick to affirm them, there is a definite pop and even rock overtone to her music. Underwood acknowledges that she has been influenced by many different singers through the years, but she was adamant as she embarked on her career journey that she be marketed in the country genre. She admits that when people listen to her albums they can probably pick out the variety of singers and songwriters who have been influences in her career, among them Roy Orbison, Shania Twain, Faith Hill, Martina McBride, Garth Books, and Reba McEntire.

"I love every kind of music and I listen to everything," Underwood told Westwood One. "I like to do things that are unexpected, not anything to offend anyone or that was morally wrong, but I love doing things that are just kind of outside my box. I think that's really fun. I never want to pigeon hole myself into 'Underwood only does good girl songs' so a song like 'Before He Cheats' was perfect for the first album, just to say 'Hey, I know everybody has the good girl image of me but I can also be an actress and be somebody different in that way.' So when we did 'Last Name,' we had already been there and it was easy to build on what we'd done before with 'Before He Cheats' and 'Flat on the Floor.' We might have gone a little further this time but that song will also be good to do onstage. I think if I was driving in my car I would so be singing that song. It's a funny story and of course it's something that I would never do and never be caught doing or anything like that, which is what makes it so fun because it's so out of character for me. It's completely not believable but it's fun anyway."[14]

While Underwood has millions of fans, judging by her record sales, there are always those who attempt to classify country music and are not happy with anyone who steps outside the boundaries of what they consider to be country. It's not a new controversy—Eddy Arnold once jokingly said that when he went to New York to record, and the producer used strings on his country record, he was almost not allowed to come back to Nashville. Swing forward a few years, to when pop star Olivia Newton John won the Country Music Association's (CMA) Female

Vocalist of the Year. The late Roy Acuff, known as the King of Country Music, flubbed her name as he announced the award. A year later, Charlie Rich, himself a rockabilly singer turned country star with a definite pop twist, burned the paper that confirmed that folk/pop/country singer John Denver was the CMA's Entertainer of the Year. After the infiltration of these pop icons into country music, a group of country entertainers established an organization in protest of the integration of these types of singers into country music.

No one seemed to mind when Ray Charles recorded a country record, *Modern Sounds of Country and Western Music*, in the 1960s. They didn't protest when Hank Williams's "Lovesick Blues" crossed into the pop charts or Patsy Cline's "Walkin' after Midnight" did the same a decade later. Jim Reeves was basically a pop singer in the country world, and there were many cries of irreverence when Garth Brooks brought rock elements into his live show. These men and women might have stretched the boundaries of country music, but they brought many fans to the genre. The same is true today of singers like Carrie and her contemporaries Taylor Swift, Kellie Pickler, and Rascal Flatts. Additionally other *Idol* contestants have found their way to country, including Pickler, Bucky Covington, Josh Gracin, Kristy Lee Cook, Phil Stacey, and Danny Gokey. Like Underwood, they came with a built-in fan base from their performances on the television show.

The truth of the matter is that country music is and always has been more than three chords, though its practitioners have worked hard to maintain the truth in its lyrics. Every decade has had its protesters picking on someone they consider to be straying too far from country's roots. Faith Hill, Garth Brooks, and Shania Twain were hot topics in the 1990s. In the first decade of the 2000s, the so-called culprits are Underwood, Taylor Swift, and Rascal Flatts.

One of the persons most outspoken about Underwood in 2009 was the man who is the epitome of country music, George Jones. Jones has always been hard-core country, from his early Texas roots that date back to his first recordings in the 1950s. His fans have remained loyal to him throughout his career, which included a few years in the 1980s when he became known as "No-Show Jones," due to his inability to handle liquor and drugs while keeping up with his tour schedule. Country icon, the late Waylon Jennings, once said, "If we could sing like we'd want to, we'd all sound like George Jones." Pure country singers like Jones, Merle Haggard, and even Johnny Cash had trouble getting airplay on radio as country music stretched its pop boundaries. Cash reestablished himself with the 20-something group of music fans before he passed away, but he never garnered additional airplay on country radio. Jones and Haggard have remained outspoken about their music not being played, as country radio's playlists were shortened to a very pop-oriented Top 40 format.

When a writer from the Associated Press (AP) asked Jones in late 2009 what he thought about today's country stars, the singer was quick to cite Underwood as one of the singers he claims has stolen the identity of true country singers. "They had to use something that was established already, and that's traditional country music. So what they need to do really, I think, is find their own title, because they're definitely not traditional country music."[15] He went on to say that there were quite a few people who hoped that the traditional country music would return to the airwaves, a subject about which he is also very outspoken.

Shortly after those comments were made to the Associated Press, Jones found himself at a party honoring Dolly Parton. Another of the invited guests at the music industry event was Underwood. Jones immediately walked up to Underwood and began to explain his statements to the AP, but he was interrupted by the Oklahoma songstress, who told him that she never thought his statements were meant as a criticism of her. Jones went on to explain to *The Tennessean,* saying, "I don't want anyone to think I'm against anybody."[16] He added that he was trying to make the point that most of today's contemporary country music is nothing like the traditional country music that he grew up on or that was popular at the time of his entry into the country genre.

When Underwood was competing on *American Idol,* she was quoted as saying that no matter what happened with the show, she wanted to be a country artist. Her best scenario was that even if she came in second, fifth or eighth, a country label out of Nashville would have seen her on the show and would be interested in signing her as a country act. Joe Galante, former chairman of Underwood's label, Sony Music Nashville, is adamant that she is a country act with no aspirations to go pop or rock. He told *Billboard* magazine, "Underwood has positioned herself as somebody that cares about this format deeply. She is a country artist. She's made it very plain. I think it [her success] all hit her like a ton of bricks in the first couple of years and now this year [2009] has been easier. Underwood has grown up a lot considering she got dropped into this format on her head, not on her feet, and people were standing on the sidelines going, 'You're not really country, you're a TV show star.' I think she's impressed the heck out of people by her reverence for country music."[17]

Underwood's wildest dream did come true. Not only did she win the *Idol* competition, she is one of country music's most celebrated newcomers, releasing CDs on one of the genre's major labels. The singer is well on her way to having a long-term career in country music, embracing the possibility with enthusiasm and honoring the music's roots with her inclusion as a member of the Grand Ole Opry family. She has not discredited the music's image with negative headlines in newspapers and televisions shows across the country. Just as Jones and his peers have their place in country music, so does Underwood and her contemporaries. Country music is one of the few genres that opens its arms to everything from bluegrass on one side to Americana and western music on the other. Underwood is finding her own niche and thrilled to have her music be a part of the country music family.

While Underwood has always declared herself to be a part of the country music community, she also admits that she's not the very traditional country singer. "I make country music but I make country music that everybody can like, which is very important to me," Underwood told the newspaper *NewsAsia*. "I'm not the kinda person who makes remixes of songs, like pop versions, and like different versions. I'd rather just make great music that hopefully everybody could be really into and can really enjoy."[18]

NOTES

1. Vernell Hackett, Carrie Underwood Interview, Westwood One, October 2, 2007.

2. Ibid.

3. Ibid.

4. Ibid.

5. Ibid.

6. Ibid.

7. Ibid.

8. Ibid.

9. Ibid.

10. Ibid.

11. Ibid.

12. Deborah Evans Price, Cover Story, *Billboard*, October 16, 2009.

13. Ibid.

14. Vernell Hackett, Carrie Underwood Interview, Westwood One, October 2, 2007.

15. Caitlin King, "George Jones: New Country Music Needs a New Name," Associated Press, November 2, 2009.

16. Peter Cooper, "George Jones Isn't against Anybody," *The Tennessean*, November 10, 2009.

17. Price, Cover Story.

18. Asha Popatlal and Hasnita A. Majid, "Carrie Underwood Is a Flavour with a Lasting Taste," *Channel NewsAsia*, October 19, 2009.

Chapter 9

WE'RE YOUNG
AND BEAUTIFUL

When a singer reaches the popularity that Underwood has reached in her four short but extremely successful years in country music, it is sometimes hard to maintain relationships. Many an artist will admit that they find little free time to keep in touch with family, much less maintain friendships or form new ones. Not only does the singer have to find time to write songs and go into the studio to record, she has concert tours and television appearances to do as well as media interviews, special appearances, and more. It's no wonder that Underwood says she spends very little time in her house in Nashville nor does she find much time to visit her hometown of Checotah, Oklahoma.

Another part of the equation is when an artist is popular and successful, people around them tend to be "yes" people—yes that song is wonderful, yes you sound great on that recording, yes the concert was awesome, and yes you are beautiful and wonderful and talented. After awhile, the star begins to believe what everyone is saying, even though they may know deep down in their heart that it is all a mirage. As the saying goes in the industry, "Never believe your own press!" The entertainers who read it and believe it, whether good or bad, are the ones who lose touch with reality.

One other thing Underwood has to deal with is the constant assault on her privacy from well-meaning fans and the folks who may not have all her interests at heart. Tour buses drive by her house in Nashville on a daily basis; it is their purpose to show music fans who come to Nashville where all the singers live and where they record. If the singer walks out to get her mail in sweats she may be met with a group of fans waving out the windows of vehicles driving slowly by her place of residence. She also has to deal with paparazzi that stick a camera in her face at every opportunity, not so much in Nashville but especially when she is out with husband Mike Fisher or out on the town with the girls in Los Angeles or New York City. Often when Underwood is shopping or at dinner with friends, people will recognize her and think nothing of coming up and talking with her and asking her for her autograph. It's an imposition on her private time and it's a hard adjustment to make for someone who has come to worldwide fame so quickly. Sure, when a person decides to become a public figure, they open themselves up for this type of life. However, it's not often that they fully understand just how hard it's going to be to have any free time or private time of their own when their life is suddenly an open book for every journalist, blogger, photographer, and music fan.

In the December 2008 issue of *Elle* magazine, Underwood acknowledged that she knew what she was getting into before she became a celebrity. "I knew what I was signing up for, and I'm not complaining at all. I've learned how to deal with it, and my life is great, I'm a happy person. What are you going to do? Give it all up? No!"[1]

Nevertheless, the singer says it's a little disconcerting to be out and know she's constantly being watched and perhaps even judged. "It's odd to think that even if I'm going out with my friends or something like that, people are watching me," Underwood admitted to *Billboard* magazine. "I'm constantly thinking, 'Should I put my drink down?' or something like that. It's really awkward to think that somebody is going to snap a picture of me dancing and then they'll say I'm a party girl, which I'm not. So you have to think about everything you do and either you decide to go ahead and do it anyway or decide to realize that everybody is going to talk about it the next day and try to be a little on your guard."[2]

The singer recalled a time in 2008 when a couple of people recognized her in a Victoria's Secret retail store and wouldn't stop following her. "I have a weird thing about that," she told *Entertainment Weekly*. "I have problems going into a store like that. I'm a private person, and I don't want people knowing what kind of underwear I like. It's creepy! But these girls followed me the whole time, and I'm like, 'Man, they see every single pair of underwear I'm putting in my little shopping bag!' Just say something. Say hey, I'll say hey, it'll be good, and then we can both continue shopping."[3]

Even Underwood's parents are going through some of the same things in Checotah that the Carrie is at her home in Nashville. Her mother told Westwood One that sometimes she will walk outside the family's home and a group of fans will be driving by, or will be parked in their driveway. "Honestly we are trying to just keep our lives as normal as we can. We mow our own yard and we haul in our hay, but we do see people drive by our house and point at us you know, and there we are sitting on the porch drinking a glass of tea. They might stop and ask if this is where Carrie lived and when we say she's not here they say 'Oh we couldn't be that lucky but could we take a picture?' So we just say yes you can and then we go in the house."[4]

Underwood seems to have a group of people around her who help to keep her grounded. She and her mother remain very close, and she is friends with peers Kellie Pickler, Miranda Lambert, and Taylor Swift. It's also a plus that she and her band members get along, as they are together for extended periods of time when she goes on tour. She told Westwood One Radio that they all have their own personal interests, but they also have things they like to do together when they are on the road, so it's "kind of like a nice little family there. The guys get kind of rowdy and we team up against them sometimes, but everybody's cool and we all get along great."[5]

Despite all the public scrutiny, Underwood maintains that she can still live somewhat of a normal life. She sometimes hangs out with pals Taylor Swift and Kellie Pickler when all three are in Nashville, and she continues to find that she can go out on her own. "I still love to go home, still like to do normal things," she says. "I live in Nashville, so I don't have paparazzi following me around. I go to the grocery store. I go to the mall. I try to live my life like a normal person would, as best I still can."[6]

Not only does Underwood strike up friendships with her peers, she also likes their music. When asked who the most underrated artist is in country music, she immediately replied it was Miranda Lambert. "She gets attention and people know who she is, of course, but I'd lose an award to her any day. I just think she's super talented and really sweet and fun. I think she deserves more accolades. She gets some, but she deserves more."[7]

Underwood does keep her fans informed about new records and tours through her Web site, http://www.carrieunderwoodofficial.com. She's not a big fan of social networks like Twitter and Facebook, where many artists post messages for fans in addition to the information they convey from their own personal Web sites. The singer told *Billboard* magazine, "It just sounds like organized stalking to me. I talk to my fan club members and I blog, and they know what's going on. But as far as Twitter, I'll be in a restaurant and I'll get home and somebody tweeted and they talked about what I ordered and what I was wearing. In some cases, that could be dangerous, because you don't want everybody to know where you are every second of every day. It's a wee bit of an invasion of privacy."[8]

The Checotah, Oklahoma, native has a great network base to work from when it comes to staying grounded. Not only is she best friends with her mother, her two sisters and father love her as the family member who left Checotah to compete on *American Idol*, not because she is now rich and famous. "I had a very happy childhood full of the wonderful simple things that children love to do," Underwood reveals in her record company bio for *Carnival Ride*. "Growing up in the country, I enjoyed things like playing on dirt roads, climbing trees, catching little woodland creatures and, of course, singing. I loved to be able to run around outside and mom and dad never had to worry about me."[9]

Underwood told *Country Weekly* that she is one of those people who has been lucky enough to have great people around her to help keep her grounded. "I think that's something that a lot of people can kind of loose their way a little bit if they don't have people that will tell them the truth and I talk to my mom a lot. I love my parents. I have a great family and good friends that will be honest with me and will let me know if there's something that I'm doing is inappropriate."[10]

The singer is quick to credit her mother with providing her with the necessary upbringing to help her develop into what she calls a "good person." She told Westwood One, "I think the most important thing I've learned from both my parents is just how to be a good person. They worked really hard to make sure that me and my sisters had a really good life and all the opportunities in the world and we grew up right and the best thing I can do is pass that on to my kids some day. It's nice to have my mom around now, too, while I'm going through all these changes in my life."[11]

Underwood has recorded several songs in honor of her mother. On *Some Hearts* she recorded "Don't Forget to Remember Me," written by Morgane Hayes, Ashley Glenn Gorley, and Kelley Lovelace. Although she didn't have a hand in writing it, the singer has described the tune as an account of what was going on in her life at the time, with a daughter asking her mother to remember her as she goes off to handle whatever it is that she needs to do at the moment. On her 2009 album *Play On*, she recorded "Mama's Song," which she cowrote with Kara DioGuardi, Marti Fredrickson, and Luke Laird. Underwood says it started out as a song about a mother giving her daughter over to her husband at a wedding, but then she decided she wanted it to be more universal than that—perhaps a mother seeing her daughter off to college for the first time, or to a new job in another city.

Underwood told *Billboard* that she was shy when she embarked on her *American Idol* journey, and she understands that it would have been easy for anyone in her position to go nuts when everything started to happen. Her saving grace has been the fact that the people who knew her before she became a household name treat her like the Checotah native that they've always known. "People around me treat me like a human being and a normal person. If I get out of line my mom is going to tell me I'm out of line, and I have friends around me that if I start acting like I'm a big thing, then they will put me in my place real quick. I hope I don't do that often but if I do, I know they'll tell me. They just treat me like anybody else. I just have a job that more people see me doing but it's still a job and I'm a human being like everybody else."[12]

The singer acknowledges that her shyness can sometimes be taken the wrong way. She adds that she's the type of person who processes everything as it's told to her. She told AOL's theboot.com, "I think sometimes [because] I'm quiet and shy, I can be misperceived and taken as I'm not very nice. I think somebody has to be really close to me to understand. . . . I really need to work on that because I don't want people to just know what they see. I would really like to, of course, keep the super-private stuff super-private but kind of let people into my world. The new album [*Play On*] has done that a little more, and I'm going to keep working on it myself because I would like people to know about me as a person."[13]

In an interview with *Allure*, Underwood says she was a "ditzy kid growing up. All I did was yap, and I always got in trouble for talking in class. Which is funny, because I don't talk much now." The singer goes on to admit, "I'm horrible in crowds. I just get so nervous. This happened to me when I was in high school, before all of this [fame]. I would start having panic attacks in Wal-Mart. I do not like shopping in close quarters and stuff like that; I just can't do that."[14]

Outside of family, Underwood is friends with former *American Idol* contestant Kellie Pickler and country music sensation Taylor Swift. The two have been spotted at Nashville Predator hockey games and just hanging for a girl's night out. In the December 2008 *Elle* magazine cover story on Underwood, Pickler is quoted as saying, "She's already proved she can sing her ass off. She can sell records. She can write. She can do it all. She's so talented, and she's sweet and beautiful—all in one package. For anyone to say anything bad about her, I think they're just jealous."[15]

Soon after her *American Idol* win, Underwood told the Web site "It's My Life" just what she looked for in a friend. "They have to be trustworthy and a person who, if it's two in the morning and you really need to talk to someone, will pick up the phone and be glad to talk to you."[16]

The singer gained a whole new network of friends when she became a member of the Grand Ole Opry on May 10, 2008. Earlier in the year, on March 15, one of Underwood's favorite singers, Randy Travis, surprised her as she ended her hit "All-American Girl" during an appearance on the Opry stage. "I've been asked by the management to come out here and ask you if you would like to be the next member of the Grand Ole Opry."[17]

"Oh my gosh, that was so amazing, and I couldn't have imagined it from a different person. And everybody here kept a tight lip," the singer said of her invitation, which she promptly accepted. At a backstage press conference, the singer was still teary-eyed at the thought of becoming an Opry member. "It's what we used to watch when I was little, at my

Grand Ole Opry member Randy Travis, left, invites Carrie Under-wood to be the next member of the Grand Ole Opry at the Grand Ole Opry House in Nashville, Tennes-see, March 15, 2008. (AP Photo/ Josh Anderson.)

grandparents' house. It was where I learned about people from the past to the present in country music as well as newcomers coming into country music. It's been a huge part of country music and it's wonderful to me that I'm going to be an official part of it, not just showing up and singing every once in a while," Underwood concluded. "My grandparents loved the Opry so much and passed that love on to me, and hopefully in some way I'll pass that love on to other people."[18]

Grand Ole Opry manager Pete Fisher said Underwood was asked to be a member because the management felt she would perpetuate the Opry and its legacy for years to come. Travis said it was fun to watch the singer's reaction to his invitation when she realized why he was onstage with her. Grand Ole Opry member and fellow Oklahoman Vince Gill proclaimed the invitation one of the smartest things the Opry had done in a long time.

Underwood walked through the backstage area prior to her induction on May 10, commenting on the Opry and other members who had inspired her. "The Opry has so much of my respect, and it always has. To walk up and down the halls backstage and see pictures of the women who have come before me and made their mark, and to think my picture will be on these walls, now is just a really cool thought."[19]

Fellow Oklahoman Garth Brooks flew into Nashville to officially welcome Underwood and induct her as the Opry's newest member. Recalling his induction, Garth told Underwood that he cried like a baby on the night he became a member. He proceeded to tell her, "You will get numerous awards from the CMA, the ACM and the Grammy but nothing lasts as long or will be more important than this award here tonight."[20]

Once again in tears, Underwood acknowledged his comments. Taking the award, she said, "Before I walked out onstage to sing you told me 'You're gonna walk out there and sing and come back a Grand Ole Opry member.' This has a very special place in my awards case. Thank everyone at the Opry for having me as part of your family because it seems like a great family to be a part of. It means a lot to me and I promise I'll do everything I can to make you not regret it. I am so blessed."[21] Backstage after her induction she said, "The award they gave me says, 'Hey, you're a part of the family.' It means a lot to me because the Opry is the heart of country music, the church, the sacred place, the super-elite club that says you love this music."[22]

It sounds as though Underwood has found her network of friends and family who support her but at the same time make sure she knows they're not going to give her any slack when it comes to her celebrity. Those are the people everyone needs in their life to ensure that they never forget their roots and never try to portray themselves as something they aren't.

Should these friends find themselves needing to talk to Underwood and she's not around, they can just fly to New York City and visit Madame Tussaud's, where a wax figure of the singer is now enshrined alongside *American Idol*'s Simon Cowell, Beyonce, President Barack Obama, Madonna, President Bill Clinton, Princes Diana, Rachel Ray, and Marilyn Monroe. Underwood is wearing a replica of the pink sequined dress that she had on when she received her first CMA Female Vocalist of the Year Award in 2006. She carries a small clutch bag and stands with one hand on her hip. The likeness is eerily close to the real thing.

In order to facilitate the making of Underwood's likeness, a group of people who sculpt the figures came out to visit the singer while she was on tour. She said she had to be still for a long time while they measured her and then took lots of pictures. The figure, which was unveiled in October 2008, is located in the museum's VIP Room.

November 11, 2008, found Underwood hosting the CMA Awards with former touring partner Brad Paisley. Even though her primary job was as cohost for the evening, the singer managed to pick up several awards, including her third consecutive Female Vocalist of the Year award. In accepting the honor, she told the audience, "I got here in an unconventional way and you guys didn't have to accept me at all."

Underwood closed the year with several Grammy nominations. The Checotah native was nominated for Best Female Country Vocal Performance, for "Last Name." Her vocals on Stephen Schwartz' and Alan Menken's "Ever Ever After" from the movie "Enchanted" was nominated for Best Song Written for Motion Picture, Television or Other Visual Media.

Singer Carrie Underwood poses next to her wax figure for the unveiling at Madame Tussauds in Times Square on Oct. 22, 2008. (AP Photo/Peter Kramer.)

In an interview with the *Tulsa World,* Underwood denied that she was reaching for the same goals as veteran entertainers Faith Hill, Martina McBride, and Reba McEntire, who have achieved success outside of country music. "No, I don't have goals like that," Underwood told the newspaper. "I just do what I do and hope that I can keep doing it. If stuff like that happens, then it's awesome. But if not, then that's fine, too."[23]

Underwood pointed out that she and her management team have never made a conscious effort to reach the pop market. Her biggest crossover hit was the renegade tune "Before He Cheats," the story of woman getting back at the man who cheated on her by bashing his pickup truck with a baseball bat. It charted on *Billboard's* Hot 100 pop chart. "We were told upfront that it was too country and that we needed to change the music on it so it sounded more poppy. I'm not willing to do that. I remember growing up and listening to these (country) songs that I loved, and they were such great songs. Then it always seemed like people—and I don't want to use this word in the wrong way—but they dumbed-down the song and put some stupid synthesizer, drums [prerecorded] loops on it that I really thought cheapened the song to make it fit into another format."[24]

The Checotah native was fortunate to have the backing of the millions of viewers who watched her on *American Idol* to soar to country and pop popularity so quickly, selling 11 million albums in three years. "I was lucky," admitted Underwood, "because I got to reach a lot of different types of music listeners through 'American Idol' and was lucky enough to get a fan base of people who didn't necessarily listen to country music at all."[25]

NOTES

1. Dan Crane, "The Girl in the Fantastic Bubble," *Elle,* December, 2008.

2. Deborah Evans Price, "Country Star Underwood Enjoys Fast-Moving 'Ride,'" *Billboard,* September 6, 2007.

3. Dave Karger, "Carrie Underwood: A Very Private Idol Speaks Out," *Entertainment Weekly,* October 26, 2007.

4. Pam Green, Carrie Underwood Interview, Westwood One Radio Network, November 12, 2008.

5. Ibid.

6. Eric Celeste, "Carried Away," *American Way*, September 1, 2008.

7. Ibid.

8. Deborah Evans Price, Cover Story, *Billboard*, October 16, 2009.

9. Carrie Underwood Bio, http://www.biography.com/articles/Carrie-Underwood-16730308, 2009.

10. Deborah Evans Price, "Carrie Underwood: How I've Changed," *Country Weekly*, March 23, 2009.

11. Pam Green, Carrie Underwood Interview.

12. Price, Cover Story.

13. Deborah Evans Price, Carrie Underwood Interview: 11 Questions, www.theboot.com, http://www.theboot.com/2009/10/21/carrie-underwood-interview-11-questions/, October 21, 2009.

14. Alexandra Jacobs, "Finding Her Voice," *Allure*, April 2010.

15. Crane, "The Girl in the Fantastic Bubble."

16. Carrie Underwood Bio, It's My Life, *PBSkids.org*, http://pbskids.org/itsmylife/celebs/interviews/carrie.html, February 2006.

17. Carrie Underwood Grand Ole Opry Invitation, Stage of Grand Ole Opry House, March 15, 2008.

18. Ibid.

19. Carrie Underwood Grand Ole Opry Induction Ceremony, Backstage Grand Ole Opry, May 10, 2008.

20. Ibid.

21. Ibid.

22. Ibid.

23. Larry Rodgers, "Carrie Nation: Let's Call It a Meteoric Ride," *Tulsa World*, December 14, 2008.

24. Ibid.

25. Ibid.

Chapter 10

ALL AMERICAN GIRL

Carrie Underwood started 2009 with more awards, this time from the 35th annual People's Choice, held on January 7. Underwood took home the prize for Favorite Female Singer, Star under 35, and Country Song for "Last Name." She soon found that she was nominated for the Academy of Country Music awards in three categories. On February 11, 2009, the Academy announced her as nominee for Entertainer of the Year, Top Female Vocalist, and Video of the Year for "It's Just a Dream," with winners to be announced at the 44th annual ACM Awards on April 5 in Las Vegas, Nevada.

Underwood went on to capture the Entertainer of the Year award from the Academy, the first time a female had that honor since the Dixie Chicks in 2000. She is only the seventh female to claim that award, joining the Dixie Chicks, Loretta Lynn, Barbara Mandrell, Reba McEntire, Dolly Parton, and Shania Twain. She also took home Female Vocalist. "I've had a lot of good moments in the past four years. This one takes the cake," the singer said as tears came to her eyes when she accepted the award. "Thank you God, thank you fans, thank you to ACM for nominating me in the first place. I never thought I'd be nominated and never thought I'd win. I'm shaking. I don't know what to say."

Underwood was inducted into the Oklahoma Music Hall of Fame on September 17, 2009, along with Rocky Frisco and Ramona Reed. She performed at the ceremony, which was held at the Muskogee Civic Center, 405 Boston St. in Muskogee. She joins other inductees including country music pals Vince Gill and Toby Keith, along with Wanda Jackson, Merle Haggard, Hank Thompson, the All-American Rejects, and David Gates of Bread.

Frisco is a Tulsa Sound cofounder who has played piano for some of rock's biggest artists including J. J. Cale and Eric Clapton. Reed performed with Bob Wills & the Texas Playboys, yodeling her way to fame with the famous Texas fiddle player. She also played the Grand Ole Opry, performing with Hank Williams Sr., Roy Acuff, and Minnie Pearl. She continues to play with the Texas Playboys and another Texas band, Asleep at the Wheel.

Especially sweet for Underwood was the fact that also honored on the same evening was C. H. Parker, with the Governor's Award. Parker was the music instructor and director at Northeastern State University in Tahlequah who for many years coordinated the university's summer country music show, *Downtown Country*. Underwood was a part of that show when she attended classes at NSU.

During a press conference prior to the Hall of Fame induction, the 26-year-old Underwood said, "I look at my life every day, and I'm in awe. Everything that's happened has been a gift from God."[1] She went on to say that to have such an amazing state behind her and the other inductees was a great feeling. She said a lot of people ask her why there are so many successful artists from Oklahoma. "I say, 'It's just who we are.' I am grounded in my life because of where we came from, because of how we were raised and where we were raised."[2]

Although she was being honored, the singer was called on to perform, and she was an instant success as she sang her hits, "So Small," "Last Name," "Wasted," "All-American Girl," "Flat on the Floor," "Jesus, Take the Wheel," and "Don't Forget to Remember Me." She surprised the crowd with her rendition of a Motley Crue hit, "Home Sweet Home," while the audience clapped, danced, and yelled its appreciation. Later that year, Underwood donated lyric and music sheets from her hit song, "I Ain't in Checotah Anymore." She also gave the Hall of Fame a framed, autographed picture and a plaque acknowledging the organization's "dedication to Oklahoma's historic contributions to music."

On November 3, 2009, Underwood released her third album, *Play On*. Its debut single, "Cowboy Casanova," written by Underwood, Mike Elizondo (who also worked as producer on the disc), and Brett James, was released on September 14, 2009. The tune because the fastest rising single of her career. The week it came out the song sold 110,236 downloads, making the singer the only solo country artist to have a debut single achieve more than 100,000 in sales. She sang the song during her induction into the Oklahoma Music Hall of Fame on September 17, 2009. It has been confirmed by the RIAA as a Platinum single for the singer.

The writers on this song brought a little-known and an unknown to the table for Underwood. James is a successful country writer who cowrote her debut single, "Jesus, Take the Wheel." Elizondo comes from the world of rap, having collaborated previously with Eminem and Dr. Dre. He brought the melody to Underwood and James and they wrote the lyrics. Underwood has said the song is not putting down the guy trying to pick up girls in the local bar, just a warning to women that they might run into such a Casanova should they venture into such a setting. A subsequent video has Underwood and her entourage of dancers having a good time as they dance across the television screen, eventually spurning the Casanova, who watches from the shadows.

"Cowboy Casanova" debuted on the *Billboard* Hot Country Song chart at number 26 on September 19, making it the fifth-highest debut by a female artist on the chart. When it climbed into the top 10 a month later, it gave Underwood the distinction of being the first female solo artist to have 10 top 10 hits on the country chart in the 21st century. Close behind her are Faith Hill and Martina McBride with nine each. "Cowboy Casanova" reached number one on November 21, giving Underwood her eleventh number one song, and giving her the distinction of having the most top 10 hits by a solo country female singer in the first decade of 2000. The tune also charted in *Billboard*'s Hot 100, climbing to 11 the second week it was out.

One interesting thing that happened with "Cowboy Casanova" is that the tune was played on a Seattle, Washington, radio station before its official release date. The song then made its way online on September 2, 2009, causing Underwood's record label to release the official version on her *YouTube* channel on September 3. Record labels set up elaborate promotional campaigns around the release of a single record, so having it leaked onto radio and the Internet even a week ahead of time could have had negative consequences. Fortunately for Underwood, that didn't happen, and it turned out to be one of the best singles of her career.

Underwood's second single from *Play On* was a definite change in subject matter for the singer. While "Cowboy Casanova" was a playful song with a lighthearted feel to it, "Temporary Home" was much more heartfelt and insightful. Underwood cowrote this single too, along with Luke Laird and Zac Maloy. Underwood had the idea for the song, which takes the title phrase and turns it into three different situations in which a person is in their "Temporary Home." In a press release from her publicist, the singer said she has always seen the song as uplifting. "It's hopeful, and each person in each story, in each different place in their life, knows that things are going to be okay." The video for the song was beautifully done, going back and forth between performances by Underwood, and following her on a cab ride through a city as she reaches her final destination to tell a loved one goodbye.

"Temporary Home" was released December 14, 2009, and became her 12th number-one single on March 2010, making the climb in just 18 weeks. Underwood is the only *American Idol* winner who has achieved 12 number-one singles. Prior to its release, the song was available exclusively on iTunes beginning October 20, 2009. The single made its debut on the *Billboard* Hot Country Songs chart at number 48 on December 12, 2009. The tune also was on the *Billboard* Hot 100 charts.

In the biography put out by her record company, Underwood talks about "Temporary Home." "This is a world so big it can break your heart. It just seems like there are so many problems. What do you do? Where do you start? Well, there are opportunities every day, so many things around you where you can make a difference. Sometimes it's the smallest thing—the person in this song had just 36 cents, you know?—and I'm really anticipating being able to do some good with this song."[3]

Underwood cowrote 7 of the 13 songs on *Play On*, a major step forward in her songwriting career. "Temporary Home" was the fifth single that she cowrote that climbed to number one. That's a far cry from the young woman who declared in 2006 that she wasn't sure if she could write, but she'd love to try her hand at it. "Because of my songwriting I feel like somebody can listen to this album and get more of a sense of who I am," she says in her record company biography for *Play On.* "They can listen to certain things and think, 'This is really sincere. This is really emotional. She was a writer on it, so this comes from something that was deep inside of her heart.' I do feel like people can get to know me a lot better from 'Play On'."[4]

The third single from *Play On* was "Undo It," written by Underwood, Kara DioGuardi, Martin Frederiksen, and Luke Laird. The tune was released on May 24, 2010. The singer made an appearance on the season finale of *American Idol* on May 26, where she performed the song. This was the last time Simon Cowell made an appearance as a judge on the show. Underwood also sang "Undo It" at the CMT Awards on June 9, 2010. The song became a number one single for her on the *Billboard* Country Digital Songs chart but peaked at number six on the *Billboard* Country Songs chart.

The singer continues to show growth and maturity on her third album. She's more confident as both a songwriter and in her performance of the songs she chose to record. Underwood admits in her record company bio that there's maturity in the album, but she says she also keeps it fun for her fans. "There's a little more mature subject matter on certain songs for sure, but I like to think I'm still young enough to keep the fun and the sass and things like that. I'm also in a good place where I do feel a lot more grown-up, more confident in my writing and in my ability to open myself up a little bit more."[5]

While she looks at various aspects of the world and the people who inhabit it, she takes a wide look at love's ups and downs. Although she's married to professional hockey player Mike Fisher, she admits that she's seen her share of what she sings about. "I've seen a lot in the dating world," she says in her record company bio, "and it's not one-dimensional, where I'm in love all the time or hate men all the time. I've been everywhere in between, and through my own experience or that of friends, I've seen every kind of guy, and I think some of these songs capture the everywhereness of being a woman."[6]

Play On sold 317,695 copies its first week of release, replacing Michael Jackson's *This Is It* as the number one album in the country. This gave her the distinction of being the only country act in Nielsen Sound-Scan history to achieve first-week sales of more than 300,000 units on each of their first three albums. Interestingly enough, the distinction extends to *American Idol,* where the season four winner has become the first contestant to launch three albums in a row above the 300,000 mark. *Some Hearts* has sold more than seven million and *Carnival Ride* has topped three million.

Underwood told *Billboard* magazine that she didn't feel the pressure for this album that she did on *Carnival Ride.* After the success of her debut *Some Hearts* CD, she said she knew the sophomore album had to do very well for her to continue her career in music. "I want to be somebody in the music business, not just somebody that [people say], 'Oh, yeah, five years ago she won that. Where did she go?' So making [*Carnival Ride*] was pretty stressful, but on this one I feel like I'm home. I'm in the music business. When people mention names like Kenny Chesney and Keith Urban and Brad Paisley, sometimes my name is in there too."[7]

Joe Galante, former chairman of Sony Music Nashville, Underwood's label, feels *Play On* represents a growth for the singer/songwriter, sonically, vocally, and from a lyrical standpoint. He also feels it is a more personal album for her. "We had more fun on the last album with some of the things that she was writing. With 'Play On,' there is a balance between the fun Carrie and also one that is revealing more about herself and her views about life."[8]

The album earned the highest first-week sales of the year for any solo country artist, and the best release-week total for a female artist in any genre in 2009. Digital sales climbed to 62,848 copies sold, marking it as the best-selling digital album debut in 2009. Underwood also held down the number one slot on *iTunes* as that site's top-selling album in all genres during release week. The music video for the tune hit the number one spot on CMT's *Top Twenty Countdown* for more than five weeks, and three weeks at the top of the video countdown on Great American Country Television (GAC).

When Underwood began choosing cowriters and producers for the new disc, there was some speculation that she was making a move to pop music, especially when she chose Elizondo as a producer. She maintained that she is just recording music that is one part of country music's wide open window. In an interview with the Associated Press, she explained, "I loved Alan Jackson and Brooks & Dunn, those were the people that really first made me love country music. Then there were people like

Bryan White who were like coming on the scene. And he was like one of the people that was like 'OK, they don't have to all sound like this.' People can sound all kind of ways. And he was young and hot."[9]

She went on to say that people often tell her they didn't like country music until they saw her on *American Idol*, and now they have gone to other country music concerts. "And it's wonderful that we all kind of have our place in country music and we all pull listeners in for different reasons, and because of that we can hear everything."[10]

Underwood says she thought about what people might think when they saw she used producers like Max Martin and Mike Elizondo. "Everybody kind of flipped out over Elizondo, who I really like. They're like, 'He's a rap producer.' And it's like, well, yes, he has done that, but he's also worked with Nelly Furtado and Pink and Fiona Apple. I'm just another name he's adding to his resume of all different kinds of music."[11]

She was adamant that she was not moving away from country music. "I love what I do. And let's say 'Cowboy Casanova' crosses over, it's going to cross over as it is—fiddles, steel and all. Growing up I never liked it when people would have a country song and then change it for a different format."[12]

When Underwood's first album, *Some Hearts,* was released, she was in New York City for the 2005 Country Music Association Awards. As with the release of the debut album, the singer once again found herself in New York City on the first-day release of *Play On.* The new disc gained major national exposure, as the performer cohosted the 43rd annual CMA Awards with Brad Paisley from Nashville. She then went back to New York City, where she made her first appearance on *The Tonight Show with Conan O'Brien* on November 16. She also visited on *Jimmy Kimmel Live!*, *Ellen DeGeneres*, *The Late Show with David Letterman*, *Good Morning America*, *Live! with Regis and Kelly* and the *American Music Awards*. She also was a guest on *In the Spotlight with Robin Roberts: Bright Lights. Big Stars. All Access Nashville.* The Arts and Entertainment network (A&E) also debuted "Biography–Carrie Underwood."

Underwood and Brad Paisley were asked to once again cohost the annual CMA Awards, held on November 11, 2009, in Nashville. The singer was nominated for Female Vocalist, along with fellow Oklahoman Reba McEntire and now Oklahoma resident Miranda Lambert, along with Taylor Swift and Martina McBride. Underwood was also nominated with her hero, Randy Travis, for Vocal Collaboration for their rendition of "I Told You So."

Underwood hosted her first major television special on December 7, 2009, "Carrie Underwood: An All-Star Holiday Special" on Fox. Her guests included Dolly Parton, Brad Paisley, actress Christina Applegate, *American Idol's* David Cook, and her dog Ace. Underwood said that Parton is one of her favorites. "Oh, my gosh. She's one of my idols and I get to sing with her. Having people like her, that I've always looked up to, I've always respected, and also some of my friends, it was a lot of fun."[13]

While talking about the special with the *Tulsa World*, Underwood also took time to talk about some favorite Christmas memories. "Growing up, basically we don't have too many traditions as a family but we always celebrate on Christmas Eve and Santa would come on Christmas morning," she said. "We had these old records I would always play. It was just like a choir or something. I have them now. Thank God my Mom didn't throw them away! It makes me think about Christmas."[14]

Underwood remembers that her best Christmas present ever was a television set, given to her by her parents when she was seven. "I remember I was little and I wanted a TV so bad," said the singer. "There wasn't a box underneath the tree big enough to have a TV in it. So I was kind of disappointed. My mother had wrapped up the remote and it was like, whatever, the smallest TV you could possibly get, but it was my TV."[15]

Food is an obvious part of the Underwood family holiday. "Goodness, my mom always makes like a broccoli cheese casserole and we do like potato casseroles and stuff like that. Just whatever is meat-free, I can load on my plate. I'm not a picky eater. I just love food."[16]

Underwood ended 2009 with the news that her debut album *Some Hearts* had been named *Billboard* magazine's Top Country Album of the Decade. Her single "Before He Cheats" was the only female solo single that made a showing in the magazine's Top 20 Hot Country Songs of the Decade.

In October, Underwood visited Asia for the first time. She performed at the grand opening of Singapore's newest shopping mall, ION Orchard, on October 16. Her showcase in Singapore was her first public performance in an Asian country, and Underwood told Channel NewsAsia that she hopes to be back soon. "I would love to [come back here]!

It was so much fun. People were singing along with me and I was surprised! I mean, country music I know is not that big outside the U.S., so coming here and seeing people singing along was a real treat!"[17]

In December the entertainer announced her "Play On Tour" for 2010. She visited 45 cities from March through May, taking Craig Morgan and Sons of Sylvia as her special guests for the duration. Members of this trio are longtime friends of Underwood and were featured on the song "What Can I Say" from her *Play On* CD. Once again the tour was sponsored by Vitaminwater.

In a press release from her publicist announcing the tour, Underwood said, "I am getting so excited about next year as we are currently working through all the big plans for the tour. I cannot wait to perform new music and see familiar faces across the U.S. and Canada!" She also told *Billboard* magazine, "It (the tour) is going to be bigger. It's going to be awesome. We're pulling out all the stops." She added that she jokingly told her management team, "I don't need to make any money, let's just do this. Let's just step it up. I know everybody is going to say, 'Oh, my gosh. This cost what?' But, shoot, we can come back next year with an acoustic tour. This year let's just go for broke."[18]

The singer says she loves live performances and has never missed a show. "People can always do more than they think they can do. Everybody's had to work when they don't feel well, and I have to remember that my fans don't know that I am sick," she told Westwood One. "I might not feel very well, but once I hit the stage I feel 100 times better. I just go out and do the best job I can do, and when it's over I feel better for doing it. But as soon as I get off stage, though, I'm totally exhausted."[19]

Although Underwood loves performing, she admitted to *Elle* magazine that the traveling to and from shows is not fun for her. "I don't know how people do it. It's tiring. It's hard. Right now I do a lot because I have no reason not to. I don't have a husband or kids. If I go home, I'm home by myself. I have no reason not to be on the road, no reason not to just get out there and do everything right now, while I'm young enough to, while I can enjoy it. But I think when I get a little older, I definitely want to slow down, just because it's very stressful. It's hard on your body, hard on your mind, hard on your emotions."[20]

While she loves the studio, Underwood definitely enjoys being on stage in front of her fans. She told *CMA Close Up* "I like the intimacy of the studio and hearing how everything evolves from the demo to the finished product, but there's nothing like being in front of the fans. Especially now, they come to see me, and they give off a great energy. They're happy to be there and I'm happy they're there."[21]

Underwood found out in mid-December 2009 that her debut album, *Some Hearts*, was named *Billboard* magazine's album of the decade. The disc sold more than 10 million copies in the United States and Canada. Her image also graced the cover of *The World Almanac and Book of Facts 2010*. She was pictured with Chicago White Sox hurler Mark Buehrle and President Barack Obama. The information-packed book was first published annually in 1868. It is listed as America's top-selling reference book of all time, having sold more than 80 million copies in those more than 240 years.

Underwood had a great start for 2010 by winning Favorite Country Artist on the People's Choice Awards, hosted by Queen Latifah. She was also nominated for Favorite Female Artist, an all-genre honor that went to her friend Taylor Swift. Underwood's former tour mate, Keith Urban, took home the Favorite Male Artist award.

Underwood took part in the tribute to the late Michael Jackson that was part of the 52nd annual Grammy awards on January 31. She performed alongside Celine Dion, Jennifer Hudson, Smokey Robinson, and Usher for the performance in 3-D. This was a first for the Grammys, and millions of 3-D glasses were given out at Target stores for fans to watch these artists perform "Earth Song." The tune was originally planned to be part of Jackson's "This Is It Tour." She also picked up her fifth Grammy, Best Country Collaboration with Vocals, for "I Told You So" with Randy Travis.

Underwood made her acting debut on March 1, 2010, guesting on the television show *How I Met Your Mother*. The singer played the part of Tiffany, a pharmaceutical sales person and love interest for Ted, played by Josh Radnor.

The singer continued to find success with her album sales. On January 12, her *Carnival Ride* CD was certified triple-Platinum, for three million in sales. Two days later, *Play On*, her newest release, was certified Gold and Platinum simultaneously, for sales of one million units sold.

For someone who likes sports as much as Underwood, singing the National Anthem at the Super Bowl would be an awesome experience.

The singer was invited to do just that for Super Bowl XLIV, which pitted the Indianapolis Colts against the New Orleans Saints, who had never been to a Super Bowl before. The game took place at Sun Life Stadium in Miami, Florida, and New Orleans took home the victory for the first time in the team's history.

Underwood joined a list of prestigious celebrities when she appeared on *Sesame Street*, the longest-running children's TV show in the United States. A character was created especially for her, dubbed Carrie Underworm, and the singer recorded "The Worm Anthem" for the show. The song proclaims, "I'm pleased as punch to be a worm," emphasizing the need to be happy as the person you are. The episode began airing February 11 on PBS.

Underwood also landed her first movie role in 2010. She will play a supporting role as a church youth leader, Sarah Hill, in *Soul Surfer*, the real-life story of one-armed surfing champion Bethany Hamilton. Hill is a youth counselor at Hamilton's church, whose friendship, support, and encouragement was a major reason the young surfer was able to make the comeback she did in the surfing world.

Other stars in the movie include AnnaSophia Robb, who portrays 19-year-old Hamilton, who lost her arm in a shark attack when she was 13. Dennis Quaid and Helen Hunt are Hamilton's parents. Lorraine Nicholson portrays surfer Alana Blanchard, and Kevin Sorbo stars as her father, Holt Blanchard, both of whom were with Hamilton when the attack occurred. *Soul Surfer* is produced by Mandalay Vision/Brookwell McNamara Entertainment/Life's a Beach Entertainment. It is a Sean McNamara Film production distributed by Affirms Films, a Sony Pictures Entertainment Company. Filming began in February 2010 on Oahu's north shore in Hawaii. *Soul Surfer* is scheduled to be released in 2011.

The singer received six nominations on March 2, 2010, when the nominees were unveiled for the Academy of Country Music Awards in New York on the CBS *Early Show*. Underwood was nominated for Entertainer of the Year, Female Vocalist of the Year, Album of the Year for *Play On*, and Vocal Event of the Year with Randy Travis for "I Told You So." She was also nominated as the artist and the songwriter for Song of the Year for "Cowboy Casanova" with cowriters Mike Elizondo and Brett James. On April 18, 2010, Underwood made Academy of Country

Music (ACM) history when she became the first woman to win the coveted Entertainer of the Year award twice. She was also presented with the Triple Crown award, for having won Best New Artist, Female Vocalist of the Year and Entertainer of the Year awards from the ACM.

Underwood stayed in Las Vegas the next day to tape the CBS special "ACM Presents: Brooks & Dunn—The Last Rodeo" at the MGM Grand Garden Arena. Other celebrities participating in the event were Kenny Chesney, Rascal Flatts, Reba McEntire, Brad Paisley, Keith Urban, George Strait, Taylor Swift, Miranda Lambert, and Lady Antebellum. Kix Brooks and Ronnie Dunn were presented with the Academy of Country Music (ACM) Milestone Award for their 20-year career. The duo has taken 26 ACM awards, which gives them the record for most wins in the ACM's history. Proceeds from the taping benefited ACM's Lifting Lives, the charitable arm of the Academy.

Underwood's nominations and awards continued as the year progressed. On June 9 she received the Video of the Year trophy from CMT for her song "Cowboy Casanova" as well as the Performance of the Year award for a rendition she did of her single "Temporary Home" on CMT's *Invitation Only* concert series. A week later it was announced that she was nominated for Female Country Artist in the Teen Choice Awards, scheduled for August 9.

Carrie Underwood kicked off her "Play On" tour on March 11 in Reading, Pennsylvania, and she had a few surprises in store for her fans. She said she was going for broke on this headlining tour, telling AOL's *The Boot*, "At this point, the only thing it's about is putting on a great show and we're going out with that in mind. I definitely think we have delivered." Not only does she use a bigger stage area and more lights, she takes a cue from Garth Brooks as she flies over her audience during the performance, a show addition that she describes as "really cool." She said the entire entourage was ready for the tour, which had a 55-city itinerary for 2010. "We have a lot of moving parts on the stage. . . . My band's great, wardrobe's great. It's just more. It's all of the bells and whistles and sprinkles on the cupcake." Underwood's opening acts for the tour were Craig Morgan and Sons of Sylvia.[22]

"Play On" Tour Schedule

March 11   Reading, PA (Sovereign Center)

March 12	Albany, NY (Times Union Center)
March 13	Providence, RI (Dunkin Donuts Center)
March 15	Portland, ME (Cumberland County Civic Center)
March 16	Bridgeport, CT (Arena at HarborYard)
March 19	Atlantic City, NJ (Boardwalk Hall)
March 20	Mashantucket, CT (MGM Grand Theater at Foxwoods)
March 21	Worcester, MA (DCU Center)
March 23	Hamilton, Ontario (Copps Coliseum)
March 24	Kanata, Ontario (Scotiabank Place)
March 26	Trenton, NJ (Sun National Bank Center)
March 27	Amherst, MA (Mullins Center)
March 29	Wilkes Barre, PA (Wachovia Arena)
March 31	Rochester, NY (BlueCross Arena)
April 1	Pittsburgh, PA (Petersen Civic Center)
April 3	Pikeville, KY (Eastern Kentucky Expo Center)
April 6	Columbus, OH (Schottenstein Center)
April 7	Peoria, IL (Peoria Civic Center)
April 9	Indianapolis, IN (Conseco Fieldhouse)
April 10	Rockford, IL (Rockford MetroCentre)
April 12	Ft Wayne, IN (Allen County War Memorial)
April 13	Saginaw, MI (Dow Events Center)
April 14	Lansing, MI (Breslin Student Events Center)
April 23	Grand Rapids, MI (Van Andel Arena)
April 24	Toledo, OH (Lucas County Arena)
April 25	Cincinnati, OH (US Bank Arena)
April 27	Richmond, VA (Richmond Coliseum)
April 28	Charleston, WV (Charleston Civic Center)
April 30	Fayetteville, NC (Crown Coliseum)
May 1	Columbia, SC (Colonial Life Arena)
May 2	Augusta, GA (James Brown Arena)
May 4	Tallahassee, FL (Tallahassee County Civic Center)
May 5	Pensacola, FL (Pensacola Civic Center)
May 7	New Orleans, LA (Lakefront Arena)
May 8	Lafayette, LA (Cajundome)
May 10	Beaumont, TX (Ford Park Events Center)
May 12	Austin, TX (Frank Erwin Center)
May 13	Corpus Christi, TX (American Bank Center)

May 15	Tucson, AZ (Tucson Arena)
May 18	Fresno, CA (SaveMart Center)
May 20	Sacramento, CA (ARCO Arena)
May 21	Reno, NV (Reno Events Center)
May 22	Las Vegas, NV (Orleans Arena)
May 29	Everett, WA (Comcast Arena at Everett Events Center)
May 30	Spokane, WA (Spokane Arena)
June 1	Nampa, ID (The Idaho Center)
June 3	Broomfield, CO (Odeum Colorado)
June 4	Colorado Springs, CO (Colorado Springs World Arena)
June 12	Birmingham, AL (BJCC Arena)
June 13	Lexington, KY (Rupp Arena)
June 15	Springfield, MO (JOH Arena)
June 17	Fargo, ND (Fargodome)
June 18	Winnipeg, MB (MTS Centre)
June 20	Saskatoon, SK (Credit Union Centre)
August 29	Highland Park, IL (Ravinia Festival at Ravinia Park)
August 31	Saint Paul, MN (Minnesota State Fair Grandstand)
September 25	Portland, OR (Rose Garden Arena)
September 27	San Jose, CA (HP Pavilion at San Jose)
September 28	Stockton, CA (Stockton Arena)
September 29	Bakersfield, CA (Rabobank Arena)
October 1	San Diego, CA (San Diego Sports Arena)
October 2	Los Angeles, CA (Hollywood Bowl)
October 3	Glendale, AZ (Jobing.com Arena)
October 6	Houston, TX (Toyota Center)
October 7	San Antonio, TX (AT&T Center)
October 9	Dallas, TX (American Airlines Center)
October 10	Tulsa, OK (BOK Center)
October 12	North Little Rock, AR (Verizon Arena)
October 13	Nashville, TN (Bridgestone Arena)
October 15	Moline, IL (i wireless Center)
October 16	Kansas City, MO (Sprint Center)
October 17	Omaha, NE (Qwest Center Omaha)
October 19	Wichita, KS (INTRUST Bank Arena)

October 20	Oklahoma City, OK (Ford Center)
October 22	Memphis, TN (FedEx Forum)
October 23	Mobile, AL (Mobile Civic Center)
October 25	Tampa, FL (St. Pete Times Forum)
October 26	Jacksonville, FL (Veterans Memorial Arena)
October 27	Duluth, GA (The Arena at Gwinnett Center)
October 29	Greensboro, NC (Greensboro Coliseum Complex)
October 30	Charlotte, NC (Time Warner Cable Arena)
November 1	Cleveland, OH (Wolstein Center)
November 3	Toronto, ON (Air Canada Centre)
November 5	Uniondale, NY (Nassau Veterans Memorial Coliseum)
November 6	Manchester, NH (Verizon Wireless Arena)
November 12	Roanoke, VA (Roanoke Civic Center)
November 13	University Park, PA (Bryce Jordan Center)
November 14	Newark, NJ (Prudential Center)
November 16	Baltimore, MD (1st Mariner Arena)
November 29	Auburn Hills, MI (The Palace Of Auburn Hills)
December 1	St. Louis, MO (Chaifetz Arena)
December 2	Evansville, IN (Roberts Stadium)
December 4	Des Moines, IA (Wells Fargo Arena)
December 5	Sioux Falls, SD (Sioux Falls Arena)
December 7	Rapid City, SD (Rushmore Plaza Civic Center)
December 8	Casper, WY (Casper Events Center)
December 12	Bozeman, MT (Brick Breeden Fieldhouse)
December 14	Yakima Valley, WA (SunDome)
December 16	Vancouver, BC Canada (Rogers Arena)
December 18	Edmonton, AB Canada (Rexall Place)

While the singer planned her U.S. and Canadian tour for 2010, management was thinking international, with plans to take Underwood and her music to fans in Australia, the United Kingdom, and Germany in the very near future. "The world needs to discover Carrie Underwood, so that's something exciting to come," Underwood's manager Simon Fuller, chief executive of 19 Entertainment, told *Billboard*. "Carrie always said that she'd love to take country music to the world and that would make her very proud."[23]

For her part, Underwood is thrilled to have found a career in music. While admitting that it's not all smooth sailing, the singer told Singapore's *NewsAsia*, "Every career comes with its little problems and snags here and there but it's so much fun—I get to sing, this is my job. I get paid to sing, and I did that in my shower every single day growing up so it's really amazing to just get to do what I love and hopefully, I can do that for a long time."[24]

While Underwood loves what she does and where her career has taken her, she also loves what her career is allowing her to do for others. There's no doubt that the singer would have made major contributions to society in whatever path she chose to follow, but it is true that her celebrity allows her to do so in bigger ways. Nevertheless, Underwood is adamant that no matter what a person does with their life, they can make a difference. In her record company biography for *Play On*, Underwood says, "Everybody has the power to do something, to be a contributing force, and I would rather people look back on my life and say, 'She made the world a better place.' We can all do things like that, and I believe that when opportunities arise for you to do good, you should do good."[25]

NOTES

1. Jennifer Chancellor, "Okie Stars Inducted into State's Hall of Fame," *Tulsa World*, September 17, 2009.

2. Ibid.

3. Carrie Underwood Biography, *SonyMusicNashville.com*, http://www.sonymusicnashville.com/artists/biography.cfm?artistid=1000011.

4. Ibid.

5. Ibid.

6. Ibid.

7. Deborah Evans Price, "Carrie Underwood: The Billboard Cover Story," Billboard, October 16, 2009.

8. Ibid.

9. Chris Talbott, "A Little Bit Country, a Little Bit Rock 'n' Roll—a Little Bit More," *Tulsa World*, November 3, 2009.

10. Ibid.

11. Ibid.

12. Ibid.

13. "It's A Carrie Underwood Christmas Special," *ET Online*, http://www.etonline.com/news/2009/12/81463/, December 1, 2009.

14. Rita Sherrow, "A Very Carrie Christmas," *Tulsa World*, Dec. 6, 2009.

15. Ibid.

16. Ibid.

17. Asha Popatlal and Hasnita A. Majid, "Carrie Underwood is a Flavour with a Lasting Taste," *Channel NewsAsia*, October 19, 2009.

18. Deborah Evans Price, "Carrie Underwood."

19. Ibid.

20. "Carrie Underwood: Idol's Biggest Star on Fame, That Voice and That Other Blonde," *Elle*, December 2008.

21. Peter Cronin, Carrie Underwood's Wild Ride, CMA News Service, October 4, 2006.

22. Alanna Conway, "Carrie Underwood Reveals More 'Moving Parts' on Tour!" *theboot.com*, http://www.theboot.com/2010/03/11/carrie-underwood-tour/, March 11, 2010.

23. Deborah Evans Price, "Carrie Underwood: The Billboard Cover Story," Billboard, October 16, 2009.

24. Popatlal and Majid, "Carrie Underwood is a Flavour with a Lasting Taste."

25. Carrie Underwood Biography, *SonyMusicNashville.com*, http://www.sonymusicnashville.com/artists/biography.cfm?artistid=1000011.

APPENDIX 1: DISCOGRAPHY

* indicates number-one single

Some Hearts (19 Recordings/Arista Records)

"Wasted"
"Don't Forget to Remember Me"*
"Some Hearts"
"Jesus, Take the Wheel"*
"The Night Before (Life Goes On) "
"Lessons Learned"
"Before He Cheats"*
"Starts with Goodbye"
"I Just Can't Live a Lie"
"We're Young and Beautiful"
"That's Where It Is"
"Whenever You Remember"
"I Ain't in Checotah Anymore"
"Inside Your Heaven"*

Carnival Ride (19 Recordings/Arista Records)

"Flat on the Floor"
"All American Girl"*
"So Small"*
"Just a Dream"*
"Get out of This Town"
"Crazy Dreams"
"I Know You Won't"
"Last Name"*
"You Won't Find This"
"I Told You So"*
"The More Boys I Meet"
"Twisted"
"Wheel of the World"

Play On (19 Recordings/Arista Records)

"Cowboy Casanova"*
"Quitter"
"Mama's Song"
"Change"
"Undo It"
"Someday When I Stop Loving You"
"Songs Like This"
"Temporary Home"*
"This Time"
"Look at Me"
"Unapologize"
"What Can I Say (Featuring Sons of Sylvia)"
"Play On"

Note: All of Underwood's albums are multiple million sellers.

APPENDIX 2: AWARDS

2005

Billboard Music Awards Top Selling Hot 100 Song for "Inside Your Heaven"

Billboard Music Awards Top Selling Country Single for "Inside Your Heaven"

Billboard Music Awards Top Country Single Sales Artist

Teen Choice Awards Choice Reality Star–Female

World's Sexiest Vegetarian—PETA's annual online poll

Oklahoman of the Year—*Oklahoma Today* magazine

Rising Star Award—Oklahoma Music Hall of Fame

Artist of the Year—Spot Music Award from the *Tulsa World* newspaper

2006

CMA Female Vocalist of the Year

CMA Horizon Award

ACM Top New Female Vocalist

ACM Single Record of the Year for "Jesus, Take the Wheel"

CMT Female Video of the Year for "Jesus, Take the Wheel"

CMT Breakthrough Video of the Year for "Jesus, Take the Wheel"

CMT Female Video of the Year for "Jesus, Take the Wheel"

AMA Favorite New Breakthrough Artist

Billboard Music Awards Album of the Year for *Some Hearts*

Billboard Music Awards Country Album of the Year for *Some Hearts*

Billboard Music Awards Female Billboard 200 Album Artist of the Year

Billboard Music Awards Female Country Artist of the Year

Billboard Music Awards New Country Artist of the Year

Gospel Music Association's Country Recorded Song of the Year for "Jesus, Take the Wheel"

Inspirational Country Music Mainstream Country Artist

American Music Favorite New Breakthrough Artist (all genres)

People's Choice Favorite Female Singer

People's Choice Favorite Country Recorded Song for "Jesus, Take the Wheel"

Napster Most Played New Artist in U.S.A.

Canadian Country Music Songwriters of the Year Award to Brett James, Hillary Lindsey, and Gordie Sampson for "Jesus, Take the Wheel"

ASCAP Song of the Year, "Jesus, Take the Wheel"

Nashville Songwriters Association International (NSAI) Song of the Year for "Jesus, Take the Wheel" for songwriters Brett James, Hillary Lindsey, and Gordie Sampson

2007

Grammy Best New Artist

Grammy Best Female Country Vocal Performance for "Jesus, Take the Wheel"

(Best Country Song also awarded to "Jesus, Take the Wheel" songwriters)

World's Sexiest Vegetarian—PETA's annual online poll

CMA Female Vocalist of the Year

CMA Single of the Year for "Before He Cheats"

ACM Top Female Vocalist

ACM Album of the Year for *Some Hearts*

ACM Video of the Year for "Before He Cheats"

CMT Female Video of the Year for "Before He Cheats"

CMT Video of the Year for "Before He Cheats"

American Music Awards (AMA) Favorite Country Female Artist

AMA Favorite Country Album for *Some Hearts*

AMA T-Mobile Text-In Award

People Magazine's 100 Most Beautiful Issue

ASCAP Song of the Year to songwriters Chris Tompkins and Josh Kear for "Before He Cheats;" Most Played Songs of the Year for "Before He Cheats," "Wasted," and "Don't Forget To Remember Me" (all awards to songwriters)

2008

Grammy—Best Country Female Vocal Performance for "Before He Cheats"

CMA Award—Female Vocalist of the Year

ACM Award—Top Female Vocalist

AMA Favorite Country Album for *Carnival Ride*

People's Choice Awards—Favorite Female Singer

People's Choice Awards—Favorite Country Song for "Last Name"

People's Choice Awards—Favorite Star 35 and Under

Teen Choice Awards—Choice Red Carpet Fashion Icon Female

BMI Songwriter Awards for "All-American Girl"

BMI Songwriter Awards for "So Small" and "All-American Girl"

Forbes List of the 100 Most Powerful Celebrities

People Magazine's 100 Most Beautiful Issue

2009

Grammy—Best Country Female Vocal Performance for "Last Name"

ACM—Entertainer of the Year

ACM—Top Female Vocalist

People's Choice—Favorite Female Singer

People's Choice—Favorite Country Song for "Last Name"

People's Choice—Favorite Star 35 & Under

BMI Songwriter Award—"Last Name"

People Magazine's 100 Most Beautiful Issue

Glamour Magazine's 50 Most Glamorous Women of 2009

Inductee—Oklahoma Music Hall of Fame

Harmony Award

Billboard Award—#1 Country Album of the Decade, "Some Hearts"

2010

Grammy Award—Best Country Collaboration w/Vocals, "I Told You So" with Randy Travis

People's Choice Award—Favorite Country Artist

ACM Award—Entertainer of the Year

ACM Award—Triple Crown Award Winner

CMT Award—Video of the Year for "Cowboy Casanova"

CMT Award—Performance of the Year, "Temporary Home," on *Invitation Only: Carrie Underwood*

People's Choice—Favorite Country Artist

Grammy—Best Country Collaboration with Vocals for "I Told You So" with Randy Travis

GLOSSARY

A&R (artists & repertoire)   the person at a record label who generally is the go-to individual for an artist. It is also the division of a record label that is responsible for talent scouting and overseeing the artistic development of the artist.

Artist   a person who makes a career out of recording music, performing, and other projects within the music industry.

Billboard   a magazine that provides information to music industry personnel at record labels, publishing companies, studios, and other industry businesses. It includes charts for singles and albums in most genres, as well as news and tour information on artists in all genres. It also has an online presence.

Booking agency   the company that signs an artist in order to organize a tour for them, book them on television shows, and get them songs or roles in movies, book deals, and other related items.

Booking agent   the person assigned by the booking agency to work with the artist on a day-to-day basis to see that they get as many deals as possible.

Country Aircheck   a magazine that provides information on country music to businesses in the music industry. It includes a singles chart for country music, as well as industry information on radio news as well as on artists and the industry itself. It also has an online presence.

Gold record An album certified by the RIAA for sales of 500,000 units.

Liner notes the writing that is in the CD booklet. It could contain notes from the artist and the producer about the songs and the recording process. The notes could be written by the artist or a journalist hired to write them.

Manager a person who oversees an artist's career, overseeing the recording, concert schedule, and promotion for the artist's singles that go to radio, as well as all other aspects of their career.

Master tape a tape with the original songs recorded by the artist, kept to preserve them. A copy of this is sent to the pressing plant for CDs to be manufactured.

Mastering engineer a person who ensures that the album as a whole has the same level on each song so that the listener doesn't have to constantly change the volume as each songs plays.

Mixing engineer a person who works in a recording studio behind the board and makes sure all the musical instruments and the artist's voice are balanced while they are recording.

Nielsen SoundScan an information and sales tracking system created by Mike Fine and Mike Shalett. It tracks sales of music and music video products throughout the United States and Canada. The weekly data can be obtained via a subscription by music industry companies such as record labels, music publishers, music retailers, and artist management. SoundScan is the sales source for all of the *Billboard* charts.

Online retailer sites online that sell albums and single songs by an artist, for example, iTunes, Amazon, Wal-Mart, Target, and Barnes & Noble.

Platinum record an album certified by the RIAA for sales of one million units.

Pressing plant the place where CDs and vinyl records are made.

Producer a person who directs the entire recording process for an album for the artist.

Promoter one of two kinds of promoters in the music industry. One works with the record label to promote an artist's single record to radio to help it get more airplay. The other promoter works to advertise an artist's concerts, helping to get print and electronic media stories when the artist is set to perform in different cities across the United States. This person also buys advertising to promote the artist's concert dates.

Publicist   a person who attempts to get stories written about the artist in print and online magazines, as well as helping get them on television shows and radio interviews.

Publishing company   a company that employs songwriters to write songs, then attempts to get those songs cut by an artist on their album.

Record label   the company that signs an artist and releases albums and singles.

Recording Industry Association of America (RIAA)   the association that monitors sales by an artist, notifying them as they reach Gold, Platinum and multi-Platinum status for albums, singles, and cell phone ringtones.

Recording session   the time an artist spends in the studio recording music for the record label, or the time musicians work to get the music tracks ready for the artist to come in and record their voice with them.

Retail outlet (brick and mortar)   a physical store where fans can go to purchase a recording by an artist.

Song plugger   a person who pitches songs to artists who are recording.

Songwriter   a person who writes songs, by themselves or with other songwriters and/or artists.

Studio   the place where an artist goes to record music for their record label.

Studio musician   a person who plays a specific musical instrument, or a variety of instruments, who is called on to play during a recording session.

Track (cut)   one song on the artist's album.

FURTHER READING

Aspinwall, Cary. "Shy Down-Home Waitress Blossoms into Superstar." *Tulsa World*, October 29, 2008.

Associated Press. "Carrie Underwood has her Town Talking." http://today.msnbc.msn.com/id/7794328/#ixzz0rF1pfMRo, May 9, 2005.

Barker, Lynn. "Carrie Underwood Plays On." *Teen Music.com*, http://www.teenmusic.com/2009/11/30/carrie-underwood-plays-on, November 30, 2009.

"Best New Artist 2007: Carrie Underwood." *Grammy Magazine*, January 11, 2010.

Caplan, David, and Charlotte Triggs. "Carrie Underwood on Chace Crawford: He's Really Cute," *People* magazine, http://www.people.com/people/article/0,,20152766,00.html, October 17, 2007.

Carrie In Badgley Mischka Campaign. http://www.carrieunderwoodofficial.com/news/carrie-in-badgley-mischka-campaign, March 3, 2009.

"Carrie's Texted Breakup with Chase." *ExtraTv.com*, http://extratv.warnerbros.com/2008/04/carries_texted_breakup_with_ch.php.

"Carrie Underwood." *CMT.com*, http://www.CMT.com, November 3, 2009.

"Carrie Underwood." *CMT Insider,* http://www.cmt.com/shows/dyn/cmt_insider/113097/episode.jhtml, December 9, 2006.

Carrie Underwood Bio. *Great American Country*, www.gactv.com/gac/ar_az_carrie_underwood, April 7, 2008.

Carrie Underwood, Danny Gokey visit St. Jude kids." *USA Today*, http://content.usatoday.com/communities/idolchatter/post/2010/01/carrie-underwood-danny-gokey-visit-st-jude-kids/1, January 16, 2010.

"Carrie Underwood Has Her Town Talking." Associated Press, May 9, 2005, http://today.msnbc.msn.com/id/7794328/.

"Carrie Underwood: It's My Life." http://www.Pbskids.org, February 2006.

Carrie Underwood Record Company Web Site. http://www.sonymusicnashville.com/artists/details.cfm?artistid=1000011.

"Carrie Underwood's Wedding Dress: Girly, Simple and Glamorous." *People*, http://stylenews.peoplestylewatch.com/2010/03/31/carrie-underwoods-wedding-dress-girly-simple-and-glamorous/, March 31, 2010.

"Carrie Underwood Visits St. Jude Children's Hospital, Memphis, Tenn." *ainow.org*, http://www.ainow.org/index.php/tidbits/1747-danny-gokey-a-carrie-underwood-visit-st-jude-childrens-research-hospital.

"Carrie Underwood: What She Eats for Clear Skin and 12 Other Secrets." *Self* Magazine, January 2010.

"Carrie Underwood Wins American Idol." *Fox News*, http://www.foxnews.com/story/0,2933,157706,00.html, May 26, 2005.

Celebrities. "Carrie Underwood Engaged to Hockey's Mike Fisher." *The Tennessean*, December 22, 2009.

"Celebs Say, Carrie Underwood." *It'sMyLife.com*, February 2006.

Celeste, Eric. "Carried Away." *American Way*, September 1, 2008.

Chancellor, Jennifer. "Carrie Underwood and Beau Get Engaged." *Tulsa World*, December 22, 2009.

Chancellor, Jennifer. "Checotah's American Idol Turns Country Music Star." *Tulsa World*, October 26, 2008.

Chancellor, Jennifer. "Okie Stars Inducted into State's Hall of Fame." *Tulsa World*, September 17, 2009.

Chancellor, Jennifer. "Very Excited: Carrie Underwood at the BOK." *Tulsa World*, October 26, 2008.

Conners, Claire. "How I Lost 20 Pounds." *Shape*, February 2008.

Conway, Alanna. "Carrie Underwood Reveals More "Moving Parts" on Tour!" *Theboot.com*, http://www.theboot.com/2010/03/11/carrie-underwood-tour/, March 11, 2010.

Cooper, Peter. "Carrie Underwood Comes out of Her Shell." *The Tennessean*, November 6, 2009.

Cooper, Peter. "George Jones Isn't against Anybody." *The Tennessean*, November 10, 2009.

Coyle, Jack. "Carrie Underwood Talks about Debut Disc, Awards Show." Associated Press, November 17, 2005.

Crane, Dan. "The Girl in the Fantastic Bubble." *Elle*, November 4, 2008.

Cronin, Peter. "Carrie Underwood's Wild Ride." CMA News Service, http://www.countrymusiconline.net/carrieunderwood_cma.html, October 4, 2006.Elliott, Matt. "Carrie Nation." *Tulsa World*, November 17, 2006.

Evans Price, Deborah. "Carrie Underwood: 11 Questions." *theboot.com*, http://www.theboot.com/2009/10/21/carrie-underwood-interview-11-questions/, October 21, 2009

Evans Price, Deborah. "Carrie Underwood: How I've Changed." *Country Weekly*, March 23, 2009.

Evans Price, Deborah. "Country Star Underwood Enjoys Fast-Moving 'Ride.'" *Billboard*, September 6, 2007.

Evans Price, Deborah. Cover Story. *Billboard*, October 16, 2009.

Gallagher, Pat. "Carrie Underwood was 'That Girl' When Meeting Randy Travis." *theboot.com*, http://www.theboot.com/2009/12/02/carrie-underwood-randy-travis/, December 2, 2009.

Gleason, Matt. "Coming Clean." *Tulsa World*, March 20, 2005.

Helling, Steve. "Carrie Underwood Reveals Text-Message Split from Chace." http://www.people.com/people/article/0,,20189421,00.html, April 7, 2008.

Hyman, Vicki. "Carrie Underwood, Mike Fisher of Ottawa Senators Engaged." *The Star-Ledger*, [Newark, N.J.], December 21, 2009.

"It's A Carrie Underwood Christmas Special." *ET Online*, http://www.etonline.com/news/2009/12/81463/, December 1, 2009.

Jacobs, Alexandra. "Finding Her Voice." *Allure*, April, 2010.

Kaplan, James. "How American Idol's Carrie Underwood Went from Small-Town Girl to Big-Time Star." *Parade*, October 11, 2006.

Karger, Dave. "Carrie Underwood: A Very Private Idol Speaks Out." *Entertainment Weekly*, October 26, 2007.

Karger, Dave. "Carrie Underwood and Tony Romo: A Passing Fancy." *Entertainment Weekly*, www.ew.com/ . . . /0,20007164_20008533_20152859, 00.html, October 17, 2007.

King, Caitlin R. "Carrie Underwood Engaged to NHL Player Mike Fisher." Associated Press, http://www.newschannel5.com/global/story.asp?s=11711208, December 21, 2009.

King, Caitlin R. "George Jones: New Country Music Needs a New Name." Associated Press, http://www.cleveland.com/music/index.ssf/2009/11/george_jones_new_country_music.html, November 2, 2009.

Lofaro, Tony. "Carrie Underwood's Engagement Ring Estimated to Cost from $150,000 to More Than $1 Million." *The Ottawa Citizen*, December 23, 2009.

Logan, Cathy. "Crowning Carrie." *Tulsa World*, December 31, 2006.

Mayer, Robin. "Country Has a Home in the North." *concertlivewire.com*, http://www.concertlivewire.com/country06.htm, July 23, 2006.

"Mike Fisher: No Seranades for Carrie Underwood." http://www.people.com/people/article/0,,20314444,00.htmlMarch 3, 2009.

Nudd, Tim. "Carrie Underwood 'Couldn't Imagine' Being Married Now," *People* magazine, http://www.people.com/people/article/0,20152995_20350143,00.html, October 18, 2007.

Park, Michael Y. "Carrie Underwood Won't Cohabitate with Mike Fisher." November 28, 2009,

Popatlal, Asha, and Hasnita A. Majid. "Carrie Underwood Is a Flavour with a Lasting Taste." *Channel NewsAsia*, http://www.channelnewsasia.com/stories/entertainmentfeatures/view/1012317/1/.html, October 19, 2009.

Rocchio, Christopher. "Carrie Underwood, Tony Romo Engagement May Be Coming." *www.realityworld.com*, http://www.realitytvworld.com/news/report-carrie-underwood-tony-romo-engagement-may-be-coming-5332.php, June 12, 2007.

Rodgers, Larry, "Carrie Nation: Let's Call It a Meteoric Ride." *Tulsa World*, December 14, 2008.

Sherrow, Rita. "A Very Carrie Christmas." *Tulsa World*, December 6, 2009.

Talbott, Chris. "A Little Bit Country, a Little Bit Rock 'n' Roll—a Little Bit More." *Tulsa World*, November 3, 2009.

"Their Wedding Planning." *Hollywoodcrush.com*, http://hollywoodcrush.mtv.com/2010/01/04/carrie-underwood-says-fiance-mike-fisher-is-very-involved-with-their-wedding-planning/, January 4, 2010.

Usigan, Ysolt. "The Making of a Smart Idol: Carrie Underwood." http://www.collegebound.net/content/article/the-making-of-a-smart-idol-carrie-underwood/629/.

Vena, Jocelyn. "Carrie Underwood Says Fiancé Mike Fisher Is Very Involved with Their Wedding Planning." http://hollywoodcrush.mtv.com/2010/01/04/carrie-underwood-says-fiance-mike-fisher-is-very-involved-with-their-wedding-planning/, January 4, 2010.

Walls, Jeannette. "Carrie Underwood's Football-Star Boyfriend Is Calling for a Timeout." http://www.msnbc.msn.com/id/18537946/, June 11, 2007.

Wooley, John. "Carrie Country." *Tulsa World*, May 26, 2005.

Wooley, John. "Carrie-d Away." *Tulsa World*, May 14, 2005.

Wooley, John. "Carrie On!" *Tulsa World*, May 22, 2005.

Wooley, John. "Idol Eyes a Show at Home." *Tulsa World*, June 4, 2006.

Wooley, John. "Tracking Checotah's Carrie Underwood in her Quest to Become the Next 'American Idol.'" *Tulsa World*, March 24, 2005.

INDEX